Braja Sorensen is an Australian writer who moved to India at the turn of the century, and lives in Mayapur, West Bengal. She is the author of *Lost and Found in India, Of Noble Blood, Mad and Divine: Collected Writings, India and Beyond: Plane Reading for Part-time Babajis, Kavita: Search for Transcendence* and *Short Lives: Growing Up to Die.*

Living the Bhagavad Gita

Ancient Wisdom for Modern Life

BRAJA SORENSEN

hachette INDIA

First published in India in 2019 by Hachette India
(Registered name: Hachette Book Publishing India Pvt. Ltd)
An Hachette UK company
www.hachetteindia.com

SRD

ISBN 978-93-5195-271-8

Hachette Book Publishing India Pvt. Ltd
4th & 5th Floors, Corporate Centre,
Plot No. 94, Sector 44, Gurugram – 122003, India

Typeset in Minion Pro 11/16
by Jojy Philip, New Delhi - 15

Printed and bound in India by
Manipal Technologies Limited, Manipal

FSC
www.fsc.org
MIX
Paper from
responsible sources
FSC™ C104740

This book is dedicated to my brother, Bhima

To all my teachers, guides, predecessors and sources of inspiration

And to all the yoga practitioners who seek depth in their practice

tasmad ajnana-sambhutam
hrt-stham jnanasinatmanah
chittvainam samsayam yogam
atisthottistha bharata

Therefore, the doubts which have arisen in your heart out of ignorance should be slashed by the weapon of knowledge. Armed with yoga, stand and fight.

– Bhagavad Gita

yogena cittasya padena vacam
malam sarirasya ca vaidyakena
yopakarottam pravaram muninam
patanjalim pranajalir anato 'smi
abahu purusakaram
sankha cakrasi dharinam
sahasra sirasam svetam
pranamami patanjalim

Let us bow before the noblest of sages, Patanjali, who gave yoga for serenity and sanctity of mind, grammar for clarity and purity of speech, and medicine for perfection of health. Let us prostrate before Patanjali, an incarnation of Adisesa, whose upper body has a human form, whose arms hold a conch and a disc, and who is crowned by a thousand-headed cobra.

– *Yoga Sutras*

Contents

Part 3

Entering an Internal Practice:
The Last Six Limbs of Yoga

Introduction

WHEN MY PUBLISHERS FIRST saw the manuscript for this book, it was quite different. They asked me to make it 'more modern, more applicable, something people could pick up and use to solve their daily problems'.

And so it became just that.

The Bhagavad Gita does not really need an introduction, being the spiritual and literary masterpiece that it is. The most famous excerpt from the Mahabharata, it is a discourse that takes place before the commencement of the battle at Kurukshetra, when Arjuna, the Pandava prince, rides onto the battlefield and views the chariots and soldiers around him. Seeing that the opposing army consists of his own relatives and friends, his revered guru and even his beloved grandfather, Bhishma, Arjuna is filled with doubt and confusion and turns to his charioteer, lifelong friend and advisor, Krishna, for guidance.

Yet, while this world-famous text involves a dialogue that takes place in a battlefield thousands of years ago, it remains relevant to this day, as Krishna's teachings and divine wisdom are equally applicable today, to us, as they were to Arjuna then. The Bhagavad Gita was not spoken just for Arjuna, in a situation or environment that we could likely never relate to. Rather, Arjuna's situation resonates through the ages: he expresses to Krishna all of the things that are disturbing him, and in resolving those dilemmas for Arjuna, Krishna is answering all human beings.

This book, *Living the Bhagavad Gita*, transforms ancient wisdom into a clear understanding of life, and life as it has to be lived today, offering solutions to the myriad problems we all encounter. The topics Arjuna raises, and which Krishna addresses, are present *now*, they are ours. Yet, they have also been the same questions that people have stumbled over for centuries: Who am I? What is my purpose? Why am I in this situation? How do I overcome my problems? Who do I turn to when I am down and out? Why am I so unhappy? What is truth and what is untruth? What is love, where can I find it? What is the meaning of life? What happens when I die? And so on. The Bhagavad Gita's greatest teaching – in fact, its very essence – is that it is a manual for living. It is the ultimate guide to understanding life, love, relationships, the workings of the world, the processes of the body, mind and senses, and the nature of the soul.

So, if any of these questions sound familiar, you're holding the right book. Here, you will learn how yoga is an applicable philosophy and a way of life that will cleanse your mind, heart and body, helping you overcome the many obstacles you face, be they at home, in your relationships, in the workplace or in society.

The fundamental meaning of the word 'yoga' is union with the Divine, and that is what the Bhagavad Gita teaches – that is, in fact, the purpose of yoga. Yet, the word 'yoga' actually has many other meanings, all explained in depth by Krishna in the Gita. The understanding of yoga unfolds from the very start of Krishna's dialogue with Arjuna. It is yoga that Krishna is actually teaching Arjuna when he gives him solutions for his confusions, sorrows and doubts. While many people in today's times think that yoga just means yoga asanas, let me assure you that the truth is far from mere yogic poses! While asanas are the fourth limb of ashtanga yoga, yoga encompasses all aspects of life and living.

What many people don't realize is that the Bhagavad Gita is the original treatise on yoga, and the source of Patanjali's own teachings. While Patanjali is rightfully known as the 'father' of yoga, the source of his *Yoga Sutras* was the Bhagavad Gita and Krishna's teachings. Patanjali's texts were written around 1,700 years ago; the Gita was spoken on the battlefield of Kurukshetra over 5,000 years ago. Every acknowledged and authoritative text on yoga post-dates the epic discussion between Krishna and Arjuna.

If the Bhagavad Gita is the essence of yoga, the original treatise on yoga, you may wonder why we need to include Patanjali's *Yoga Sutras* here in this book. Let me explain. While Patanjali's book discusses the link between body, mind and soul, and how the practice of yoga affects each aspect, the Gita is a more expanded treatise on the philosophical and psychological effects of yoga, and how yoga results in a specific action and result. The Gita is also more expansive in terms of the spiritual development of the practitioner and the processes required for this development to take place. In that respect, it speaks of the more devotional aspects of yoga, specifically bhakti yoga and sadhana.

While the Bhagavad Gita explains how yoga addresses every topic applicable to life, Patanjali takes the practice of ashtanga yoga – the eightfold process of yoga and the most widely used form of yoga in the world – and elaborates in detail how every aspect of ashtanga yoga leads one from physical practice to the very basics of ethics and principled thought; it also takes one right through to the higher elements of yoga and its spiritual aspects. Patanjali describes pratyahara, the fifth limb of ashtanga yoga, as the bridge that takes the yoga practitioner from the external practice of yoga to the higher, more internal aspects of yoga's spiritual elements. Patanjali's *Yoga Sutras* and Krishna's teachings in the Gita also deal with the realm beyond the body, mind and senses. Thus, they serve as a guide to life, both materially and spiritually speaking.

In his book, *Light on the Yoga Sutras,* India's most famous modern-day yogi, Yogacharya B. K. S. Iyengar, calls the *Yoga Sutras* the 'philosophical core' of yoga. He explains that Patanjali's teachings parallel Krishna's in the Gita, and that the combined practice of bhakti and ashtanga yoga is how one learns to use the mind, consciousness and intelligence so that one is able to give form, balance and peace to the hundreds of muscles and joints in the body, to the mind and to the senses and, eventually, to the very soul.

As Patanjali took his inspiration from the Bhagavad Gita, B.K.S. Iyengar took his from the *Yoga Sutras*. In this book, these two principle treatises on yoga – the Bhagavad Gita and the *Yoga Sutras* – are combined in one simple handbook whose contents anyone can practise in their daily lives. Just as Krishna's teachings in the Gita lead us step by step to a higher consciousness and advanced practice of yoga, so Patanjali's *Yoga Sutras* take us step by step through the maturing of our thoughts, actions and behaviour, and onto the higher, more subtle elements of spiritual consciousness.

Bhakti yoga and ashtanga yoga are sciences: their application demands that those who offer guidance to others on these forms of yoga be trained themselves, qualified by the process they seek to teach, knowledgable not merely through the eyes of their own limited vision but actually empowered by the study and experience of yoga. Furthermore, they are obliged via that same tradition to acknowledge their own teachers, and not claim the knowledge they speak of to be a product of their own creation. Instead, their knowledge should be seen as part of a continuum, and a natural display of the humility required to practise yoga. This is a fundamental requirement in how to choose our teachers, and is a core element of our practice.

Despite the modern-day packaging of yoga as a honing of the physical body, this practice cannot truly be called yoga without the presence of bhakti. As I have explained above, yoga means to connect; it specifically refers to a union with the Divine. Bhakti means devotion and bhakti yoga, therefore, is not an 'optional extra', a fad, religion or any other adjective that might limit its depth, range and beauty. It is, rather, an ancient system that boldly claims the science of love – its study, understanding and practice – as both its source and as its goal, a science whose formula is devotion to the object of love which is, finally, the Supreme.

But how can love be called a science? Does 'love' even need such a label? The answer is in understanding that the practice of bhakti encompasses *all* of life. It includes every act, feeling and thought as elements of one's devotion. It incorporates speech, the written word, art, music, fabric, design, food, architecture, history, stories, literature, song and so on. Understanding that everything we do, think, feel, want or imagine, can all be part of developing our love is surely the science in which we all want a doctorate, or to be professors in all the arts and sciences that are, combinedly, called 'love' or bhakti. That's what makes it a science. Bhakti is not an emotion, yet it possesses every emotion we know; it is not a feeling, yet it absorbs and drowns all those who enter into it; it does not end, or die...it is eternal. Bhakti is conscious love in action. This is how we understand that the essential aim of yoga is love.

Both Krishna's Bhagavad Gita and Patanjali's *Yoga Sutras* encompass the process of that science. In the latter text, we have a wealth of information on the workings of the breath, organs and the muscles, and on the subtler science of the mind and psyche of the yoga practitioner. In the Gita, we are given revelations of how the knowledge of these fields directs our devotional process; we are also taken deeper into the science of devotion. Together, these two texts create the most wonderful and practical handbook on yoga.

HOW TO READ AND USE THIS BOOK

Living the Bhagavad Gita is a *practical* book, applicable to daily living. It brings to life the essence of the Bhagavad Gita and delivers it in a simple and concise way that can be taken up by anyone, regardless of religion, race or age. Each chapter also provides solutions to problems that the reader can actually apply in life.

Let's begin with how *Living the Bhagavad Gita* can be read and its wisdom experienced. This book is split into three sections:

- The first part of the book explores the basics of living a daily yoga practice.
- The second part focuses on developing a strong spiritual core that serves as the foundation for a deeper yoga practice.
- The third part provides an explanation of the physical and spiritual methods that make up one's yoga practice, in a practical and doable sense.

The first part of the book includes a clear and concise analysis of every mention of the word 'yoga' in the Bhagavad Gita, peppered with tips to help the reader practically apply what they have just read.

The second and third sections of the book offer a similarly detailed and practical guide to the sage Patanjali's ashtanga yoga process, illuminated by the wisdom of Krishna's teachings of yoga in the Gita. The second section explains the first two limbs – 'yamas', the ethical disciplines, and 'niyamas', rules of conduct, that form the foundational principles of yoga. In the third and final section of the book, we address the remaining six limbs of ashtanga yoga: asana, pranayama, pratyahara, dharana, dhyana and samadhi.

It should be understood from the start that this is a handbook, a guide to the Gita's teachings specifically on yoga and its various applications, meanings and practices. Hand in hand with the *Yoga Sutras,* we take a comparative journey through the Gita and its teachings on yoga, incorporating the philosophical and spiritual aspects of Krishna's discourse with Patanjali's elaborate detail on the specific limbs of yoga.

While every use of the word 'yoga' and all Krishna's and Patanjali's teachings embody a wealth of knowledge on philosophical matters, the purpose of this book is to guide you in understanding yoga and its applications. Therefore, while I am naturally inclined to elaborate on the broader and deeper philosophical and spiritual aspects of yoga, I will refrain from going in too deep, so we don't lose the primary focus of the book.

While reading this book, therefore, it is recommended that you have with you a copy of the Bhagavad Gita so that you might read the entire chapter that is being discussed. This will help you gain a much broader understanding of the conversation between Krishna and Arjuna. The version of the Gita I am using is *Bhagavad-gita As It is*, a translation and commentary by A.C. Bhaktivedanta Swami.[1] It is recommended that this version be used while reading, as my book uses both the translation and commentaries presented by Bhaktivedanta Swami. The quotes you will find here are his words taken from this book.

I hope my book helps you to see how life unfolds in the hands of a science whose field is love, whose formula is devotion and whose goal and result are the same as its practice: loving devotion.

---

[1] Bhaktivedanta Swami, *Bhagavad-gita As It Is*, Bhaktivedanta Book Trust, 1972.

Part 1

BHAGAVAD GITA

A Treatise on Yoga

CHAPTER 1

Meanings and Practices of Yoga

THE BHAGAVAD GITA CONSISTS of eighteen chapters. Chapters 1 to 6 address karma yoga; chapters 7 to 12 focus on bhakti yoga; and chapters 13 to 18 deal with jnana yoga. Karma refers to work; bhakti means devotion; and jnana is knowledge.

Krishna says in chapter 9, verse 27, 'Whatever you do, whatever you eat, whatever you offer or give away, and whatever austerities you perform – do that, O son of Kunti, as an offering to me.'

In other words, the goal of all karma yoga is bhakti.

In chapter 7, verse 19, Krishna says, 'After many births and deaths, he who is actually in knowledge surrenders unto me, knowing me to be the cause of all causes and all that is. Such a great soul is very rare.'

Thus jnana leads to bhakti.

Then, Krishna explains to Arjuna in chapter 6, verse 47: 'Of all yogis, the one with great faith who always abides in me, thinks of me within himself, and renders transcendental loving service to me is the most intimately united with me in yoga and is the highest of all.'

The goal of yoga, as both Krishna and Patanjali elucidate, is union with the Divine, which *is* bhakti yoga.

In chapter 8, verse 28, Krishna tells Arjuna, 'A person who practices bhakti yoga is not bereft of the results derived from studying the Vedas, performing sacrifices, undergoing austerities, giving in charity or studying various philosophical approaches. Simply by practicing bhakti yoga he attains all these, and attains the supreme abode.'

Krishna's emphasis is consistent: the practice of yoga is a process of purification of the mind, body and spirit, and this purity lends clarity to one's thoughts, actions and purpose. Patanjali refers to such practitioners as being *satyam-pratisthayam*, situated in truth, and Krishna refers to them as *tattva-darsinah*, seers of truth. Both Krishna and Patanjali teach that such people are practising bhakti yoga.

Despite the fact that the Gita presents three different streams of yoga one after the other, progressing through karma, jnana or raja yoga to reach the level of bhakti yoga is not a necessity. Why? Because bhakti yoga is not dependent on other forms of yoga. The goal of all aspects of yoga, in whatever order they are presented, is to bring practitioners to the highest yogic stage: bhakti yoga.

Therefore, you may wonder why this discourse on the elements and practice of yoga is written in the order it is, progressing from karma yoga to bhakti yoga and ultimately arriving at jnana yoga. You may also ask why the Gita doesn't just focus on bhakti yoga as the means to attain the Divine.

Krishna explains the crucial reason for all this in

chapters 9 and 12. Each person is different, and chooses a path depending on their personal needs and temperament. We are all individual souls, and each person's past, present and future are unique. The only element is that bhakti is dependent on are the individual's own level of purification, choice of spiritual path and personal determination.

Therefore, if one does not have the desire to pursue bhakti yoga, then the other systems of yoga, which also embody the elements to take one to the next level on the path of life, both materially and spiritually, can do so. For, while union with the Divine is the ultimate spiritual goal, Krishna is inviting everyone to engage in this process from any angle, be it through hatha yoga, karma yoga, jnana yoga, ashtanga yoga, raja yoga, dhyana yoga or bhakti yoga, making it possible for people walking any of these yogic paths to be able to attain its highest goal.

THE MEANINGS OF YOGA

Now we look closely at each use of the word 'yoga' in the Gita, beginning with the first six chapters. When we break down and understand each use of the word and its varied meanings, it simplifies the rather esoteric philosophy of yoga and allows us to understand and connect with its profound wisdom. It is important to note here that the term 'yoga' as a noun or verb ('yogena', 'yukta' and 'yuktena') may not be specifically mentioned in the Gita; instead, the opposing meaning of yoga is mentioned, giving the dual understanding of what it is and what it is not. Every verse in the Gita is about yoga in some way or another. The Gita, as the title of this section indicates, is a treatise on yoga.

The first chapter of the Gita doesn't specifically mention yoga. Rather, it describes the situation that Arjuna finds himself in: two armies poised for battle, with the other army made up of soldiers who are Arjuna's relatives, teachers and friends. Overcome by grief and pity, Arjuna's strength leaves him and he has no desire to fight. He sits down in his chariot and tells Krishna he cannot do what is required of him. This sets the scene for the dialogue between Krishna and Arjuna, which follows in the subsequent chapters.

The second chapter of the Gita is where it all begins, where we are introduced to one of the basic disciplines of yoga: what do we do when we are faced with a situation that overwhelms us? And whom do we turn to when confusion and fear arise, when we are vulnerable, when we feel out of control, when we need guidance and instruction, when we realize that we simply do not know the answers or have the solutions to the problems that assail us? Arjuna leads by example: he asks for guidance.

These days, it's common to have disdain for authority, or to think that we don't want or need authority or guidance. But actually, we follow authority by default every day. In fact, our entire lives are a process of accepting knowledge from authorized sources: from our parents, family members, school teachers, college professors, employers and other experts. Our lives are full of authorized moves and instructions we have to obey, from traffic lights to supermarket queues, from yoga classes to school hours for children and work hours for adults, from kindness to animals to our personal behaviour with friends, family, colleagues and even strangers. All of us follow instructions, accept authority and live according to the rules made by man and God.

While our minds may initially reject the idea of 'authority', we respond to it all the time. It is, in fact, quite rare to find a person who is hellbent on rejecting authority, who doesn't see the value in following instructions or who disrespects people simply because they are authorities.

But sometimes, we do see those who had assumed the mantle of authority stumble and fall, perhaps in the most inelegant of ways, and we question why we should waste our time seeking out those who seem to bear the same human frailties that we do. Are these really the people we should look up to and be guided by? What is the difference between a real authority and a phony or weak one who will only let us down? How do we determine the difference?

There is one question we can ask here to help us understand how to find a genuine guide. It is by seeing who *their* authority is. To whom do they give credit for their knowledge? What kind of understanding, teaching and knowledge does their teacher bear? As the saying goes, 'there is nothing new under the sun'. Everything we learn is gleaned from an existing source and, if we are genuine in our desire to live a life of integrity, we acknowledge and respect that source, as does that source, and the source before them and so it goes on. There is, thus, a recognized line of authority that knowledge comes from.

But why is authority so important in the situation Arjuna finds himself in? We know he is overcome by emotions and his mind is in turmoil at the thought of battling with his friends and relatives. Patanjali's *Yoga Sutras* teach that one of the first aims of yoga is to bring a stillness to the mind, and Krishna speaks of the importance, a balanced and calm mind. So, when we are in turmoil, we seek to still that turmoil, to achieve equilibrium and peace. Rather than reacting to his situation in that state of turmoil, Arjuna turns to Krishna, his authority, for guidance.

When we reach out to someone for help, we're not only seeking guidance and advice, but also love, affection and understanding. Arjuna knows that Krishna can give him all this. Krishna says in chapter 4 that he is speaking this way to Arjuna because Arjuna is interested in spiritual knowledge and because he is his friend. It is natural for him to turn to Krishna for guidance and accept his answers.

This is a significant moment in the Gita, for it is here that the nature of their relationship changes. Krishna, the wise and loving friend, now takes on the mantle of a teacher, a position of authority, and Arjuna accepts Krishna as his guru; this new relationship is mutually agreed upon. Krishna's teachings on yoga unfold beautifully through the larger context of their loving relationship.

Yet, before Krishna can start instructing Arjuna, he must

first guide him out of what he refers to as 'the dense forest of delusion'. In chapter 2, verses 7–9, we see Arjuna explain his dilemma to Krishna: 'Now I am confused about my duty and have lost all composure because of miserly weakness. In this condition, I am asking you to tell me for certain what is best for me. Now I am your disciple, and a soul surrendered unto you. Please instruct me… I can find no means to drive away this grief which is drying up my senses. I will not be able to dispel it even if I win a prosperous, unrivalled kingdom on earth with sovereignty like that of the demigods in heaven… Govinda, I shall not fight.'

Let us now look at the many meanings of yoga in the Gita.

Yoga Means Intelligence

Intelligence, with its varied meanings, is a subject upon which many books are written and countless discussions held. Apart from ordinary academic intelligence, there is emotional intelligence and there is the spiritual intelligence that Krishna speaks of, the kind of intelligence that encapsulates both the intellect and the emotions.

In chapter 2, verse 39, the word 'yoga' is spoken by Krishna for the first time:

esa te bhihita sankhye
buddhir yoge tv imam srnu
buddhya yukto yaya partha
karma-bandham prahasyasi

Krishna uses the term *buddhir yoga*, spiritual intelligence, and explains that this intelligence is needed to direct one's thoughts and actions in the right manner. By doing so, *karma-bandham prahasyas*, you can free yourself, that is, not be led by the mind, senses and emotions but rather by the intelligence. Krishna explains that this is the only way by which one can become free of being bound by one's actions. Academic knowledge is commendable, but it doesn't solve the problems of life. It is spiritual intelligence that tells us how to understand all the aspects of ourselves and how to function in the world. Thus, buddhi yoga is philosophy in action.

Arjuna has stated that he will not fight because his mind is overcome with sadness. He also expresses his confusion. His realization – that he has to kill his guru, his grandfather and others who are dear to him – has overwhelmed him. He cannot understand how undertaking such an action can be right. He is despondent, disheartened and sad – three things that can be combined into one word that is instantly recognized as a modern-day problem: depression. That is something that so many of us can understand and relate to.

What is Krishna's answer to Arjuna's problem? Krishna begins the process by explaining to Arjuna that yoga means controlling the senses. Through the last verses in chapter 2, Krishna gives a detailed explanation of how one suffers when he is ruled by his mind and senses, just as Arjuna is. He explains to Arjuna how his sadness stems from his misunderstanding of life and death (and he elaborates on this later on), how his lamentation is unnecessary, and how he can learn to tolerate happiness and distress in the same way he responds to the changing of the seasons. Krishna also talks about the indestructibility and eternality of the soul.

This is where Krishna introduces the concept of balance and equilibrium.

Yoga Means Balance

People are seeking balance and harmony in every aspect of life and the more chaotic our lives become, the more we desire this balance. In chapter 2, verse 48, Krishna raises the subject of balance when he tells Arjuna to be equipoised. The word he uses is *yoga-sthah*, which is a key point.

yoga-sthah kuru karmani
sangam tyaktva dhananjaya
siddhy-asiddhyoh samo bhutva
samatvam yoga ucyate

The Sanskrit word *sthah* means 'situated in', and Krishna is telling Arjuna to be 'situated in yoga', to be balanced in thought and action. He asks Arjuna to abandon his ideas of success and failure and to give up his attachment to duty. To be situated in yoga is to focus completely on the Divine: This is the way out of all troubles and the demands of the material world. This is crucial guidance, as relevant for Arjuna then as it is for us now. He says, *samatvam yoga ucyate*, such equanimity is called yoga. In verse 49, Krishna is more adamant, advising Arjuna to keep distracting or unhelpful activities at a distance by the strength of intelligence in action or, in other words, by engaging in yoga.

Krishna uses an interesting term here, telling Arjuna *anviccha krpanah phala-hetavah*, which means that those who want to enjoy the fruits of their work are 'misers'. In the beginning, one of the reasons Arjuna would not engage in battle was his grief. What was the use of his fighting, he said, if he could not enjoy the results? Although he could understand that it was his duty to fight, he told Krishna, 'Now I am confused about my duty and have lost all composure due to miserly weakness'. Krishna tells him instead that to want to carry out his duty only if he can see its benefits is a 'miserly' attitude.

So, in this example we see Arjuna's initial reluctance to act, then his acceptance of Krishna's teachings to act with intelligence rather than emotions or senses, is the clear path to his finding balance or equilibrium. Despite the dilemma Arjuna finds himself in, he teaches us how to act when we are overcome by difficulties. Although he is unable to act and unsure of what to do, he still responds with equanimity and understanding that he should seek wise counsel, take shelter in someone who *is* balanced and not attached to the outcome, and someone who is able to guide him with a cool mind and loving heart.

Now, you may wonder how you can find a trustworthy and will guide in your life?' As previously mentioned, one key element of understanding who an authority is, or who is qualified to guide us, is by knowing who *their* guide or teacher was. Knowledge is a 'descending' process. In other words, it is handed down, given to us by one who is qualified to do so. Understanding a person's base of knowledge determines for us how bona fide their wisdom is. Every day, the world over, people are creating new 'philosophies' or trying to sell us cheap cures for our problems. But real wisdom has a basis, a foundation; a wise person has a source for their knowledge and wisdom and will always speak of what they have learned from their elders, teachers, guides or gurus.

Most importantly, the Bhagavad Gita is not simply confined to history: it is a *living* guide; its teachings are timeless and apply to everyone, everywhere. 'The proof of the pudding is in the eating' they say. In other So, one has to actually try living the gita, teachings to understand their value.

TRY THIS

We can see from Arjuna's first lesson – the very basis of yoga is to distance himself from the overwhelming control of the mind and emotions. How do we accomplish this? We do this the same way Arjuna did: he paused, and while experiencing profound grief, asked his friend and guide Krishna to help him, to instruct him.

The first step in conquering any problem is to not allow ourselves to be dominated by those things that we should actually be in control of: mind, senses and emotions. Certainly they have their place, but they should never control our innate intelligence. Understanding that our distress or suffering is a product of the senses and not of the true self – the soul – is the first principle of yoga. This understanding is expanded upon in the coming chapters, but it presents itself here as the basis. So establish it as your foundation.

Whatever the problem is – large or small – just try and take a deep breath and relax. Don't let the mind and emotions overwhelm you. As you will read in the coming pages, taking a deep breath is not gratuitous advice but is a part of yoga! I am referring to pranayama or breath practice. And don't give up: immediate results may be small, but as you begin to develop 'muscle' in your thoughts and learn to respond in different ways to problems, you will begin to see more consistent results.

Yoga Means the Art of Proper Action

Here, we reach the end of chapter 2, which establishes the process of understanding when, how and why we need to turn to someone to seek counsel. This chapter also explains who is qualified to be an authority. Arjuna's intelligence has abandoned him, he is confused about what is right and wrong, good and bad, and what will bring a good result. Krishna has explained buddhi yoga, intelligence in action, and now he elaborates further:

buddhi-yukto jahatiha
ubhe sukrta-duskrte
tasmad yogaya yujyasva
yogah karmasu kausalam

Krishna says that a person who acts by the principles and practices of yoga is not burdened by the outcome or results of performing his duty. He says: *tasmad yogaya yujyasva*, strive for yoga, because it is the art of all work – *yogah karmasu kausalam.* He is conveying to Arjuna that there is no need to worry or be confused about what path to take. We have to simply strive to understand the principles of yoga, which is kausalam, the art of all work. Being conscious of why we do something, what we are actually aspiring for, is the art of action. Sometimes, we are overwhelmed by what we have to do in our lives, day to day…the small things become too much. For instance, a man or woman might work hard simply to support the family. The 'art' of that is that one is acting according to dharma, duty. To do so with a peaceful mind, and not be overwhelmed by the action itself, is kausalam.

TRY THIS

When next faced with a problem that threatens to overwhelm you, be it something traumatic or a minor irritation, stop and ask yourself one question, a question that might sound somewhat cliched these days, but is actually a rapid solution. Think about someone you know whom you admire for their qualities, specifically qualities like quietude, wisdom, having successful relationships. This person could be a relative, friend, teacher, guru or religious elder. Then ask yourself: What would they do in this situation? Even better: meet this person if you can. Further, will yourself to slow down and take control of your responses. Don't let your intelligence be overwhelmed by your anxiety.

Yoga Means Divine Consciousness

What is 'divine consciousness'? Is it something achievable by ordinary people or is it some grandiose state of being that is only accessible to saints and gurus?

As Krishna has already mentioned, we are not this body but the eternal soul. Our nature is divine and our original, pure, unhindered consciousness is divine. Even if it is layered and burdened by conditioning of all kinds, its essence is still divine. So it is not so much a matter of acquiring a divine consciousness as becoming aware of the divine self.

How do we connect with our divine self? So far, Krishna has spoken to Arjuna about who to turn to in times of trouble, how to rein in the mind and senses and how to utilize intelligence. These elements – and who to turn to, controlling the mind and senses – are key in reinstating our divine consciousness. Krishna tells Arjuna in verse 53:

sruti-vipratipanna te
yada sthasyati niscala

samadhav acala buddhis
tada yogam avapsyasi

He is saying that once the mind is no longer disturbed, a divine consciousness – a higher state of mind – is achieved. Earlier, in verse 51, he uses the term *buddhi-yukta*, meaning actively engaging the intelligence and, therefore, attaining a level of consciousness that is *amamayam*, without miseries. This is the practical definition of 'divine consciousness': a mind and intelligence that is controlled and which, as a result of that control, can focus on higher, spiritual matters. This is how buddhi yoga connects with bhakti yoga. In chapter 2, verse 53, Krishna uses the word *yogam*, saying that when the mind is no longer disturbed, it remains fixed in *yogam* – self-realization – and a divine consciousness is the result.

Arjuna is consciously acting in buddhi yoga, addressing Krishna in the mood of a submissive enquirer, and seeking guidance and wisdom. He asks his first question of his guru in verse 54: 'What are the symptoms of one whose consciousness is thus merged in transcendence? How does he speak and what is his language? How does he sit and how does he walk?' Arjuna is now seeking to know how one can free oneself from the cage of the mind and the lure of the senses, and from being subjected to the onslaught of uncontrolled emotions, so he can gain this equilibrium Krishna speaks of, this state of *amamayam*.

Krishna responds by explaining how the mind and senses can drag one down into the state Arjuna is in. Then he summarizes by saying that firstly, nothing can be given up or simply and quickly abandoned. That's not the way the senses work. Anyone who has tried to give up smoking, drinking or any other addiction knows that it is really hard to kill a desire. If it was easy, why would it ever be a problem? The mind and senses are constantly active; consequently, the things they focus on are always present. Krishna advises that instead of trying to just give up something, these lower desires must be replaced with a 'higher' purpose, which is the Divine. The term Krishna uses is *param drstva nivartate*, which means the voluntary renunciation of something of lower value for something of higher value (2:59). He adds that one who does not actively engage in the process of yoga in this way – by actively and consciously replacing those things that disturb one with other, more beneficial activities – can have neither transcendental intelligence nor a steady mind, without which there is no possibility of peace. He concludes by asking Arjuna, 'And how can there be any happiness without peace?' (2:66).

TRY THIS

By now, you have consciously prevented the intelligence from being overwhelmed, and you have meditated on the advice of someone you consider an authority on the issue that confronts you. Now we arrive at the third step. It is something Einstein explained perfectly when he said, 'If you want a different result, you must change the formula'. In other words, do something completely different from what you would normally do. Don't become upset, don't lose your temper, don't feel overwhelmed, don't resort to those 'go-to' activities that are habitual for you.

Instead, try to actively engage in an activity – be it for five minutes or an hour – that your problem has absolutely no relation to. For example, do some service at your temple or mosque; visit a lonely relative or friend; go for a walk in the park and feed the ducks; do some charity work; sit and meditate; or chant sacred mantras. Lift yourself out of the negative energy that is surrounding you and shift your focus. Change the 'formula' you normally use for alleviating your distress in times of trouble. Yoga is a process and it is clear and simple. And, most of all, it works. Try it...

Yoga Means Guiding the Mind and the Senses

Often, when we read 'how to' books or articles – how to give up something, how to achieve something – we are left feeling even worse than we did when we started to read! Such directions or guidelines can feel overwhelming, asking things of us that we simply can't do or find unrealistic. The goals in such books can also feel impersonal in the sense that they don't recognize how hard even the 'simple' things are for regular people. I have to admit that personally, I often find inspirational writings discouraging and impractical and, consequently, unhelpful.

I've sometimes asked myself if I'm being negative in

thinking this way. But the reality is that the majority of people are inspired not by mere instruction but by people who have actually suffered unfathomable trauma, loss or devastation, and have been able to overcome the obstacles in their lives. We relate to such stories of success, and learning about how these people overcame their troubles helps us in dealing with our own. In the same way, Arjuna is easy to relate to.

Krishna is consistent in his teachings, telling Arjuna repeatedly to rein in the mind and senses. You would have realized by now that doing this is key to progressing through the different levels of yoga and attaining a higher state of thought, action and being. It may be easy to say 'Oh, well, giving up such-and-such thing is easy, just control your mind and senses.' But *how* do we do that? This is the beauty of the Gita's discussion: the wealth of practical information it embodies is applicable to everyone, and can be applied by anyone.

Chapter 3 of the Gita starts with Krishna saying to Arjuna in verse 3:

loke 'smin dvi-vidha nistha
pura prokta mayanagha
jnana-yogena sankhyanam
karma-yogena yoginam

Here, Krishna explains the two paths yoga practitioners can take to try to attain the highest levels of yoga: *jnana yogena*, which is the empirical or philosophical approach;

and *karma-yogena yoginam*, the path of devotion. Arjuna expresses confusion at this. If, as Krishna has explained, intelligence is superior to being attached to what the mind thinks is right, why then does he still want Arjuna to fight? Arjuna's intelligence is telling him to take the higher road and to not fight.

Krishna's talks with Arjuna will delve more deeply into the subject of dharma in the coming chapters. But, for now, in answering Arjuna, Krishna first elaborates on the title of this chapter, 'Karma Yoga'. Then, he goes on to explain its contents, the conclusion of which is that while the mind is higher than the senses, intelligence is higher than the mind, and the soul is even higher than intelligence. From here through to the end of the first section of the Gita (chapters 1 to 6), Krishna speaks in detail on what yoga is, what it is not, and what the effects of practising yoga – internally and physically – actually are. In chapter 4, 'Transcendental Knowledge', particularly, Krishna speaks most directly on the meaning of yoga.

Yoga Means Connection with the Supreme

Though a weighty topic to consider, the subject of this chapter in the Gita can be simply understood in linguistic terms: the word 'yoga' has the same source and meaning as the English word 'yoke', which means to cause two things to be joined or linked. As I have shared earlier, both Krishna and Patanjali explain yoga as being that practice or process that leads to union with the Divine.

In the opening verses of chapter 4, Krishna begins to explain what the science of yoga is. In verse 2, he says:

evam parampara-praptam
imam rajarsayo viduh
sa kaleneha mahata
yogo nastah parantapa

Yoga is the science of being connected to the Supreme. One may ask why this word 'science' has suddenly arisen in the last chapter or two, and why yoga is considered a science. Yoga is a precise and detailed methodology that does not rely on faith, experiment or guesswork. The Oxford English Dictionary defines science as a 'systematically organized body of knowledge on a particular subject'. The subject of yoga is the self, and yoga is the science of self-realization; it focuses on all aspects of the human being: body, mind, emotions and soul. This science of yoga requires that there first be a relationship, and then that there be devotion, without which there can be no understanding of the transcendent element of the practice of yoga. Between Krishna and Arjuna, as you know by now, there is a relationship, and Arjuna is deeply devoted to Krishna. We will see Patanjali elaborate on this 'science' in the next section.

Yoga, in this modern age, is usually viewed as a popular form of exercise. We won't exactly find a group of people in a yoga studio seeking to connect with the Divine! While physical health, lithe limbs and strong muscles, and a sense of wellness are benefits that you do gain as you pursue the yogic path, these physical gains are more like side effects, for the purpose of yoga remains constant: to connect and become one with the Divine.

TRY THIS

Pray to the Divine. Really, it's that simple. Yoga is not an impersonal process or an exercise regime: it is about connecting with God. There is no smarter way to enter 'yoga' than to actually connect with the Supreme. Pray wherever and in whatever way you feel comfortable; this could be at home, in a mosque, temple or church, in a park, or in a car stuck in traffic!

Yoga Means Knowledge

Chapter 4 of the Gita is 'Transcendental Knowledge'. The topic of knowledge is an interesting one and, like intelligence, very wide in scope. But, in the end – and this especially applies to yoga – knowledge is only worth anything when it is applied. Possessing theoretical knowledge on a subject is good, but unless this wisdom is applied to life and living, what is the use of that knowledge? The word 'yoga' appears in this chapter in verse 38, when Krishna says to Arjuna, 'In this world, there is nothing so sublime and pure as transcendental knowledge. Such knowledge is the mature fruit of all mysticism. And one who has become accomplished in the practice of bhakti yoga enjoys this knowledge within himself in due course of time.'

But leading up to this, in verse 34, Krishna directly addresses the question that has arisen in the earlier chapters: who is an authority, whom do we approach, how do we understand what knowledge is and what it is not, what is right and what is wrong? He says:

tad viddhi pranipatena
pariprasnena sevaya
upadeksyanti te jnanam
jnaninas tattva-darsinah

'Just try to learn the truth by approaching a spiritual master. Enquire from him submissively and render service unto him. The self-realized souls can impart knowledge unto you because they have seen the truth.'

Krishna is saying that by doing this, one will not fall prey to the illusion that Arjuna succumbs to at the beginning of the Gita, the state Krishna referred to then as the 'forest of delusion'.

So far, this is how Krishna has used the 'yoga' to guide Arjuna: he has addressed Arjuna's initial fear and confusion; he has explained the concept of authority and the need for it; and he has talked about receiving knowledge from such authorities, which allows us to transcend our limited understanding and perceptions of the self and the world. From this state, one can then proceed to find equilibrium within and without.

TRY THIS

Till now, Krishna has given Arjuna three clear instructions on how to overcome problems:

1. *Don't let your intelligence be overwhelmed by the mind and emotions.*
2. *Ask someone you regard as wise and experienced to help and guide you.*
3. *'Act in yoga'. You can do this by being conscious of thought and action, by meditating, praying, chanting mantras and so on. The outcome is guaranteed by Krishna. Apply the knowledge you've acquired, and experience the maturing of your knowledge, its growth and development.*

Yoga Means Fearlessness

In chapter 4, Krishna talks about fear in detail. In verse 10, he tells Arjuna, 'Being freed from attachment, fear and anger, being fully absorbed in me and taking refuge in me, many, many persons in the past became purified by knowledge of Me, and thus they all attained transcendental love for Me.' In his commentary to this verse, Bhaktivedanta Swami writes, 'One has to get rid of all three stages of attachment to the material world: negligence of spiritual life, fear of a spiritual personal identity, and the conception of void that arises from frustration in life.'

The world is a scary place, so it is hardly surprising that people live in fear of so many things: losing their loved ones, terrorist attacks, natural disasters, accidents, ill health, loss of wealth, divorce and the list goes on. Then, there is a whole range of psychological fears, like the fear of taking responsibility for oneself, the fear of loneliness, the fear of intimacy. Being responsible for ourselves, and acknowledging the reality that we are ultimately alone, are realizations that can create fear in many people.

And yet, people are equally daunted by the prospect of relieving these fears through spiritual development, and fearful of the challenges of the spiritual path. Remember that the entire dialogue that is the Bhagavad Gita was born from Arjuna's fears. He was afraid to enter into battle with his relatives, afraid to kill them, afraid to dishonour his elders and afraid of the consequences of all these things. And his fears were valid: he was thinking about the death of so many, the survival of a kingdom, the detrimental effects on the generations to come, and the dharmic consequences of his actions. Who amongst us can claim we have as much to lose as Arjuna did, and display such a noble response to our suffering?

In times of fear, we need guidance, just like Arjuna did, on how to overcome fear and confusion. We may need a hand to hold, advice on how to respond to an issue or to simply be nurtured by loving counsel. In these early chapters of the Gita, the conversation between Krishna and Arjuna highlights this as Krishna deftly begins to lead

Arjuna out of his confusion and grief, showing him the power of a balanced and peaceful mind, and telling him to use his intelligence.

Verse 42 of chapter 4 is a famous verse, and my favourite verse in the Gita. Krishna says: 'Armed with yoga, stand and fight.'

tasmad ajnana-sambhutam
hrt-stham jnanasinatmanah
chittvainam samsayam yogam
atisthottistha bharata

'Therefore, the doubts which have arisen in your heart out of ignorance should be slashed by the weapon of knowledge. Armed with yoga, O Bharata, stand and fight.' This is not just a passionate plea or an instruction. Krishna emphasizes that the knowledge Arjuna has acquired should be *applied* to destroy his ignorance. Knowledge is Arjuna's most effective weapon, for ignorance is caused by fear. Armed with this knowledge, Arjuna is to use it.

In the coming pages, we will delve further into the various kinds of energies that affect our mind, intelligence and senses. We can all understand this at a basic level, that 'some days are worse than others'. There is 'something in the air' or a 'bad feeling' one gets. Krishna elaborate on this concept when he talks about the modes of material nature. These 'modes' are explained as three different levels: the mode of goodness, the mode of passion and the mode of ignorance and they impact us on a daily basis. But suffice it to say here that one of the characteristics of the mode of ignorance is fear.

In the verse above, even beyond material obstacles, problems and fears, we are being asked to delve into spiritual fearlessness, to give up the fear of a personal spiritual identity. We have a body and we have a soul. Our material identity is the body; our spiritual identity is the soul. This is the beginning of the deeper, more internal aspects of yoga's practice: the spiritual development of the self and the goal of self-realization. Understanding the differences between a material and a spiritual way of life is a process that we are now embarking on through Krishna's talks with Arjuna.

As has already been mentioned, yoga is not about making one's life better materially or about physical health or cures. Yoga means to connect with the Divine, and it is the path to spiritual understanding and awareness. Yet, as Bhaktivedanta Swamiji points out, we have a fear the spiritual learning process and developing a spiritual identity. Krishna asks Arjuna to take this knowledge he has so far learned, and use it to destroy his fear. 'Armed with yoga, stand and fight' the fears that assail us: this is what Krishna is teaching Arjuna.

What does being 'armed with yoga' mean? The term Krishna uses is *yogam-atistha*, being 'situated in yoga', which means operating at a level that is beyond the mind and senses or, in other words, being controlled by a higher intelligence; it also means being possessed of knowledge and controlling the fear, uncertainty and confusion that Arjuna began with.

Arjuna is a warrior and a prince, a man of superior

intelligence and abilities; he is described in the Mahabharata as being extraordinarily handsome – even beautiful – tall, strong, and powerful, with 'the gait of a lion'. Yet, here he is on the battlefield, overcome by fear, unable to think clearly. Arjuna is blessed with a high birth, education, beauty, power, ability and dignity. These details are important to note for us because, as I have already said, we are ordinary people looking for solutions to life's problems. If Arjuna is so qualified and noble, we assume that he be able to deal with any sort of problem. This, however, is clearly not the case, and this is what Krishna is so deftly pointing out in his talks with Arjuna. It is not hard, therefore, to relate to Arjuna.

Yet, the modes of material energy affected Arjuna and left him incapable of going on.

The Gita offers deep guidance on understanding and working with our conditioned behaviour. It is relevant that we are not asked to negate or destroy conditioning. Krishna's relationship with Arjuna stands as an ideal example of what good counsel looks, feels and sounds like.

Krishna sums up the first four chapters by teaching Arjuna that we should not be ruled by our fears. Instead, we should use the knowledge we have acquired to conquer our fears and, in doing so, experience that knowledge maturing and developing inside us so it can become an internal 'weapon' with which we can be armed in order to battle our fears and anxieties.

As it was pointed out at the start of this section, knowledge is only useful if it is applied. That is precisely what the Gita is offering us: a way to apply higher knowledge so that it aids us in our daily lives and elevates us gradually to a higher consciousness and a higher intelligence. Thus, the wisdom of the Gita is not confined to a battlefield thousands of years ago; it is, instead, a profoundly powerful guide to everyday life.

TRY THIS

Every morning, think of these three words what Krishna has uttered: 'Armed with yoga.' Every morning, think of the first three 'Try this' points that are the basis of being 'armed with yoga':

1. *Don't let your intelligence be overwhelmed by the mind and emotions.*
2. *Ask someone you regard as wise and experienced to help you and guide you.*
3. *'Act in yoga'. Dwell on these teachings and strive to be conscious of them through the day. And, when a problem arises, apply them and see the results! Make the intent to be armed with yoga.*

Yoga Means Understanding the World

It is becoming increasingly difficult to understand the world. This age of information produces a constant barrage of news – most of it bad – about the world and its inhabitants. It's hard to understand why things just seem to get worse if we are supposedly 'advancing' in our yoga practice, in our consciousness, in developing a broader and deeper knowledge of how we are affected by things.

In chapter 5, verses 4 and 5, Krishna speaks of sankhya yoga, the analytical study of the material world. He tells Arjuna that this system helps us understand the world, how it works and our position in it, and how the philosophy of knowledge helps us to understand ourselves. The purpose of philosophical research is to understand, and attain, the goal of life, which we already know is union with the Divine through the practice of yoga.

sankhya-yogau prthag balah
pravadanti na panditah
ekam apy asthitah samyag
ubhayor vindate phalam

At this point, one may ask what all this talk of philosophy has to do with yoga. Let me explain the connection. A mature practitioner of yoga is concerned not only with their own understanding of life and its problems, but also cares to understand those issues for mankind in general. In the last section of the Gita (chapters 12 to 18), the energies of the universe are discussed in more detail, at a more advanced level, but here Krishna refers to these things briefly to indicate that this is not something to be dismissed as just 'mundane knowledge'. Remember that this is a process we are working through. We might refer to things as being explained in more detail further on because it would be too much of a distraction to delve into them at this point.

Yoga Means Action

The world is a busy place and there is so much action at every level of one's being – mentally, emotionally, physically – that one can barely keep up. Therefore, the idea that yoga means 'action' may seem like a contradiction. Aren't we meant to be 'stilling' the mind, finding our inner selves, nurturing our spiritual knowledge and elevating the mind and senses?

This idea refers specifically to karma yoga, which is the practice of yoga free of attachment, without expectation of profit or gain from one's actions. Chapter 5 is a practical explanation of karma yoga. Krishna explains to Arjuna how yoga means action, for while we often consider renunciation to be an advanced stage of life, action situated in yoga is higher than such renunciation. In other words, it isn't what you do as much as *why* you do it that is important. Yoga in action is far more productive than renunciation.

Please note that we are talking about *yoga* in action, not ordinary actions. The difference between the two is that in yoga, even though one is engaged physically, one still remains aloof from the material senses, from being controlled by them, because one is situated in divine consciousness. When one is in divine consciousness, when one acts – even if these are ordinary actions of daily life – in total surrender to the Divine, then one is practicing yoga. Bhaktivedanta Swami puts this beautifully in his purport of verse 5: 'Detachment from matter and attachment to Krishna are one and the same. One who can see this sees things as they are.'

In chapter 5, verse 21, Krishna emphasizes this by saying that a self-realized person is always happy within as he is in touch with the Divine, and does not seek external fulfilment in material pleasures, including sex, which is the most powerful material pleasure there is.

bahya-sparsesv asaktatma
vindaty atmani yat sukham
sa brahma-yoga-yuktatma
sukham aksayam asnute

A person who is in surrender to the Divine is completely absorbed in joy of the Divine, and all else falls away.

TRY THIS

When something troubles us, we all have our 'go to' reactions. We might turn to anger, have a couple of shots of whisky, walk away, see a movie, or simply refuse to face the problem, pretending it doesn't exist. Next time this happens, just stop for a moment, focus on what I have explained in the paragraphs just above, and take a deep breath. Then consciously decide you won't seek out distracting activities in this moment, but

that you will just wait, be conscious of your responses, control the demand of your senses and ride it out.

Yoga Means Renunciation

I've just finished talking about how Krishna explains to Arjuna that yoga in action is far superior to renunciation, which means to be removed from the world of actions. So you might wonder how the Gita also talks about yoga as renunciation.

As you know by now, 'yoga' has varied meanings. The word, like the practice itself, covers many aspects of life, of action or inaction, thinking or not thinking, doing or not doing. At the beginning of chapter 6, in verse 2, Krishna clearly defines the word 'yoga' in the context of renunciation:

yam sannyasam iti prahur
yogam tam viddhi pandava
na hy asannyasta-sankalpo
yogi bhavati kascana

'What is called renunciation you should know to be the same as yoga, or linking oneself with the Supreme, for one can never become a yogi unless he renounces the desire for sense gratification.'

Through this chapter, Krishna explains that the process of *ashtanga* yoga, the eightfold yoga system, is a means to control the mind and the senses (verses 11–15). Yet, Arjuna tells Krishna that he finds this whole approach too much to absorb and not easy to do. He says 'the system of yoga which you have summarized appears impractical and unendurable to me, for the mind is restless and unsteady' (6.33).

In response, from verses 17 to 23, Krishna begins to specify what is to be done and what is not to be done, what being 'situated in yoga' means in terms of the discipline and what are the practices involved. For example, one has to be regulated in the habits of eating and sleeping (6:17); one has to be disciplined in mental activity and free oneself from material desires (6:18–19); one has to be of pure mind, satisfied in the self, self-realized, truthful, steadfast and free from misery (6:20–23). Thus, one becomes free and attains the highest state of perfect happiness.

As we will see in the next section of this book, these very verses make up Patanjali's foundations of yoga, the yamas and the niyamas.

Yoga Means Freedom from Pain and Sorrow

In summing up these sections on action and renunciation, Yogacharya B.K.S. Iyengar, in his *Core of the Yoga Sutras*, says, 'The meaning of yoga is to free oneself from all bonds of pain and sorrow.' While freedom from all pain and sorrow is an understandable desire, it is not the goal, he continues, but merely the foundation of a yoga practice: 'Yoga has to be practised without distress, anxiety or fear so that one can reach the zenith in yoga.'

So verses 11–23 in chapter 6, referred to above, are the actual steps and instructions on how to achieve that zenith. It isn't the physical situation we are in that defines our happiness or our release from suffering; it isn't what we are doing that decides how satisfied we will be in life. In fact, these verses teach us that regardless of what we do, or what situation we are in, the key to peace, happiness and freedom from suffering lies in our thoughts, actions and the intent for our actions – why we do what we do. If we are disciplined mentally – which is what Krishna is teaching Arjuna here – then that freedom from fear, pain and sorrow is a given.

TRY THIS

Actually, there's nothing new to try here: rather, we see how the first practical, basic applications of yoga – not to be overwhelmed by things and not to let the emotions, mind or the senses rule us – all lead to the closing verses in chapter 6, where it states that one must be pure of mind, disciplined, truthful and satisfied mentally. We are now actively involved in the process, seeing how basic steps lead to greater understanding and tangible results.

Yoga Means Equality

Another hot topic these days is equality. We are always hearing talk of gender equality and the equality of rights. But the equality that the Gita speaks of is, in fact, the equality of vision. Krishna says to Arjuna in verse 29:

sarva-bhuta-stham atmanam
sarva-bhutani catmani
iksate yoga-yuktatma
sarvatra sama-darsanah

'A true yogi observes Me in all beings and also sees every being in Me. Indeed, the self-realized person sees Me, the same Supreme Lord, everywhere.'

In this verse, the word 'yoga' is mentioned in the term 'yoga-yukatma', meaning one who, through yoga, is aware of both the self as well as the Divine. Krishna elaborates by telling Arjuna that a yogi can see the Supreme in all beings, and all beings in the Supreme. The yogi's vision is different from one who is directed by the mind and senses. That vision is one that sees that all souls are equal, despite their physical differences. This is the vision of a yogi and the spiritual understanding of 'equality'.

This is a direct explanation of what we have been learning so far: the physical practice of yoga elevates the mind and senses and, in such an elevated state, one can connect to the Divine. As a result, despite one's surroundings or actions, one is internally content and peaceful. Again, I emphasize that yoga is a practice that one must *do* to attain this state of contentment. We don't start out at this level; we practice in order to reach here.

Yoga Means Self-realization

So far, Krishna has been instructing Arjuna, who has been listening intently, absorbing the instructions being given to him. In doing this, he is performing 'yoga in action' and using intelligence. Now, as we move further in chapter 6, the dialogue between the teacher and the disciple starts. Arjuna asks Krishna questions. This is a point to be noted. To object or to argue with information/knowledge we are given is not a dismissal of another's expression or any kind of disrespect, but evidence of an engaged intelligence. Krishna never admonishes Arjuna for questioning him.

In verse 34, Arjuna lays out his concern about the difficulties of the yoga process he has learned so far from Krishna. He says, 'For the mind is restless, turbulent, obstinate and very strong, O Krishna, and to subdue it, I think, is more difficult than controlling the wind.' In response, Krishna reiterates what he has said earlier:

asamyatatmana yogo
dusprapa iti me matih
vasyatmana tu yatata
sakyo 'vaptum upayatah

'For one whose mind is unbridled, self-realization is difficult work. But he whose mind is controlled and who strives by appropriate means is assured of success.' Arjuna should not be overwhelmed by the mind but learn to take control of it. Yes, Krishna agrees, it is difficult work, but it is certainly possible through detachment and suitable practices, as given in verse 35.

Arjuna asks Krishna a significant question here, and it is something that can easily occur to us as well: What is the fate of someone who fails in this difficult yoga process? What if one has tried to do this, but reaches the end of life without having achieved this goal?

In chapter 6, verse 41, Krishna uses the term *yoga-brastah* to explain that the inability to achieve the goal does not mean the person has failed. Earlier, in chapter 2, verse 4, when Krishna is speaking about acting in knowledge, he says to Arjuna, 'In this endeavour, there is no loss or diminution, and a little advancement on this path can protect one'. Now, he elaborates and says that if one does not achieve the goal of yoga in this lifetime, he will take birth again in the home of a saintly, pious or prosperous person so that he can continue his journey on the path to perfection in yoga.

In chapter 6, verse 44, Krishna sums up the fate of one on the path of self-realization by saying, 'By virtue of the divine consciousness of his previous life, he automatically becomes attracted to the yogic principles, even without seeking them. Such an inquisitive transcendentalist always stands above the ritualistic principles of the scriptures.'

But Krishna goes on to elucidate his point even more beautifully. In verse 46 he says, 'A yogi is greater than the ascetic, greater than the empiricist and greater than the fruitive worker. Therefore, O Arjuna, in all circumstances, be a yogi.'

The last verse of chapter 6 sums up the first six chapters of the Gita. From Arjuna's confusion, distress, hopelessness and despair, to Krishna's instructions on what the soul is, how the senses and mind function and how they control a person, to equilibrium and a divine consciousness, and finally to this point of self-realization and absorption in the Supreme, Krishna concludes in verse 47:

yoginam api sarvesam
mad-gatenantar-atmana
sraddhavan bhajate yo mam
sa me yuktatamo matah

'And of all yogis, the one with great faith who always abides in me, thinks of me within himself, and renders transcendental loving service to me – he is the most intimately united with me in yoga and is the highest of all. That is My opinion.'

TRY THIS

Read verse 41 again: there is no such thing as failure. Yoga is a process, and here you are, reaching the end of the first six steps of practically implementing the core principles of yoga in your mind, actions, thoughts, responses and heart. Yoga is a practice, and when we practise something, it becomes second nature. And second nature then becomes first nature.

In summary, we can see how these previous pages are a 'fleshing out' of the main points of this chapter:

1. *Don't lose your intelligence or let it be overwhelmed by the mind and emotions.*
2. *Ask someone wise, senior or more qualified for guidance, or think of what they would do in your situation.*
3. *'Act in yoga'. Find a way to connect yourself to the Lord through prayer or meditation. The outcome is guaranteed.*
4. *Every morning, think of the meaning of the being 'armed with yoga'. It will change your day.*
5. *Don't react, don't rely on your external 'crutches' to get you through what arises: just pause, think of the practical steps given to Arjuna by Krishna, and learn to flow.*
6. *There is no such thing as failure.*

CHAPTER 2

Living the Philosophy of Yoga

IN THE FIRST SIX CHAPTERS of the Bhagavad Gita, Krishna lays down the foundation of yoga. He discusses the mind and the senses and how to control them, and how to avoid the pitfalls of illusion and conditioned behaviour. He teaches Arjuna how to be a yogi in all situations.

In chapters 7 to 12 of the Gita, bhakti yoga is focused upon. Since bhakti, according to both Krishna and Patanjali, is the ultimate goal of yoga, these chapters are at the heart of the Gita, forming the core of all that has gone before and all that comes after.

In these chapters, the use of the term 'yoga' is more direct and descriptive than in the previous six chapters.

Yoga Means Being Conscious of God

As Arjuna is beginning to realize now, Krishna *is* the 'Supreme' or 'Divine' that he was previously referring to in the third person. Why is this a revelation? As we know from the Mahabharata and the earlier part of the Gita,

Krishna and Arjuna are lifelong friends. Krishna has a close personal relationship with Arjuna and his brothers, Kunti and Draupadi. He has always been a part of Arjuna's life, and their bond is strong. So, for Arjuna to realize that his lifelong friend Krishna is the Supreme Lord is definitely a revelation to him.

One may ask how Arjuna does not know that Krishna is the Supreme Lord. As the Vedas teach, in scriptures like *Srimad Bhagavatam* and elsewhere, there are different rasas – moods – through which one can develop a relationship with the Lord. These rasas are santa (neutral), dasya (servant), sakhya (friendship), vatsalya (parental), and madhurya (conjugal or intimate). While these rasas are mostly self-explanatory, it should be added that santa rasa means that one is fully devoted to the Lord but in a neutral capacity, without feelings associated with any sort of relationship.

Arjuna's relationship with Krishna is sakhya rasa, that of friendship. When the Lord detects that rasa in a person, as Krishna did from the very beginning of his relationship with Arjuna and his brothers, he encourages that rasa and reciprocates. Till now, the rasa has been one of friendship. Consequently, Arjuna is, at the moment, somewhat blind to Krishna's true identity. Thus, the revelation of Krishna being the Supreme Lord is the beginning of his understanding of who and what Krishna is. This topic is covered in full in chapter 11.

Now, in the first verse of chapter 7, Krishna refers to himself for the first time as the Lord. This is the beginning of Arjuna's understanding of who Krishna really is, and what the goal of yoga is.

In this verse, we see how Krishna leads Arjuna as well as the reader to the understanding of his true nature.

sri-bhagavan uvaca
mayy asakta-manah partha
yogam yunjan mad-asrayah
asamsayam samagram mam
yatha jnasyasi tac chrnu

'The Supreme Personality of Godhead said: "Now hear, O son of Pritha, how by practicing yoga in full consciousness of Me, with mind attached to Me, you can know Me in full, free from doubt."'

The guidance for Arjuna is that practising yoga in full consciousness of him, Krishna, with the mind attached only to him, will result in *asamsayam*, a mind free of doubt. But what does it mean to 'know him in full', and what does it have to do with yoga?

As Krishna teaches throughout the Gita, and Patanjali instructs in his *Yoga Sutras,* the goal of yoga is union with the Supreme. This is also bhakti yoga. B.K.S. Iyengar wrote, 'All yoga leads to bhakti'. The Vedas define bhakti as 'loving devotion' which is, like buddhi yoga, yoga in action. While buddhi yoga utilizes intelligence, bhakti is even higher: it is love manifested – in thought, speech and action.

So, we see how yoga means union with the Divine, and how

the goal of yoga is love. This is bhakti yoga in action: actively and consciously engaging in the practice of yoga to be able to experience loving devotion to the Supreme.

This is a completely different mood from the first six chapters, where we were introduced to Arjuna's doubt and confusion. Here, Krishna emphasizes that once Arjuna knows the purpose of being armed with yoga, 'nothing further shall remain for you to know'. This gives a clear understanding of the title of chapter 7 of the Bhagavad Gita, which is 'Knowledge of the Absolute'.

There are few mentions of the word 'yoga' in chapter 7. Krishna's focus in this chapter is on explaining to Arjuna in detail his divine nature, which he does for over 20 verses. He says that everything rests upon him 'like pearls on a thread'. He explains how he is the taste of water and the light of the sun and the moon; he talks about how he is the syllable 'Om' in the Vedic mantras, and also the sound in ether and the ability in man. He says that he is the original fragrance of the earth, the heat in fire, the life of all that lives and the penances of all ascetics. He teaches that he is imperishable and supreme.

In fact, these expressions of his powers, his supreme abilities and his qualities are a wonderful poetic meditation on the 'knowledge of the absolute' or learning about the Divine. They are not simply his 'qualities'. They *are* him. They are not separate from him, nor sourced from elsewhere, nor different from him. And this is possibly one of the most succinct explanations of how we, as human beings, differ from the Divine. We acquire qualities and they become our second nature; his qualities are who he *is*.

TRY THIS

We have already understood what it means to be armed with yoga. Elaborating on that, we have here a poetic description of many of the things that surround us on a daily basis, for example, 'the light of the sun and the moon' and 'the sound in ether'. All the things that Krishna speaks of can be seen by us either as an obstacle or the manifestation of his qualities, whether its the hot summer sun and traffic jams or all the things that Krishna refers to when he describes his own nature. By extension, we can see the Divine in everything around us. Training our thoughts to respond to all things, therefore, is a natural yoga meditation, and will help strengthen and expand our yoga practice.

Yoga Means Knowing Krishna

As I have explained about, the qualities Krishna posses are the very embodiment of his divine nature. Moving on, Krishna is the source of all things, including yoga and its processes.

Further, the process of reaching the goal is yoga, and as has been stated previously, the goal of yoga is union with the Divine, who we now know is Krishna. Thus, he is also the goal of all things. He tells Arjuna that those who cannot accept this absolute knowledge – that he is the Supreme Lord and the goal of all yoga – will experience him differently, in that they will perceive him to be an ordinary mortal.

Krishna reiterates this in the concluding verse of chapter 7, when he says that those who are in full consciousness of him, those who know him to be 'the governing principle of the material manifestation' can think of him at the time of death and attain the perfection of yoga, which is to unite with the Supreme.

TRY THIS

We now start to understand that the physical practice of yoga is simply a vehicle by which we enter the spiritual nature of yoga, the meaning and purpose of which is to unite with the Supreme. Therefore, we now consciously engage in yoga with the understanding that it leads to a divine union, and that everything we have learned so far is to help us achieve this. In summary:

1. *Be conscious of the Supreme's qualities and nature. This is the beginning of the journey to meet the Divine.*
2. *As a conscious yoga practice, meditate on the qualities that Krishna reveals of himself, and remind yourself that such meditation, along with the asanas, is yoga in action.*
3. *Remember that 'all yoga leads to bhakti'. Every aspect*

of yoga is, as Krishna has explained in detail, part of the process of attaining the supreme goal of union with the Divine.

Yoga Means Attaining the Supreme

Krishna uses the word 'yoga' in two verses early on in chapter 8. In verse 8, he tells Arjuna that through *yoga-yuktena*, meditating upon him, one can reach him:

abhyasa-yoga-yuktena
cetasa nanya-gamina
paramam purusam divyam
yati parthanucintayan

In verse 10, Krishna says that through *yoga-balena*, the power of yoga, one attains him:

prayana-kale manasacalena
bhaktya yukto yoga-balena caiva
bhruvor madhye pranam avesya samyak
sa tam param purusam upaiti divyam

It is significant that Krishna uses the word 'balena', which means strength. This indicates that continued work through one's life is required to attain the goal of yoga at the time of death. One cannot suddenly decide to attain the Supreme at the time of death without practising yoga throughout one's life.

The words 'yukta' and 'yuktena' are repeated throughout the Gita, both being the verbal forms of yoga – to practise. A more thorough examination of the understanding of 'practise' is given at the end of this first section.

In verse 12, Krishna speaks of *yoga-dharanam*, being situated in yoga. This is achieved, he tells Arjuna, by detachment from all sensory engagement, closing the doors of the senses and focusing the mind. Once one is situated in this *yoga-dharanam* then, as he says in verse 13, by chanting 'Om', one attains the Supreme as the soul leaves the body.

Again, in verse 14, Krishna emphasizes the constancy of the practice of yoga when he tells Arjuna that those who fix the mind on him without deviation will attain him because of their *nitya-yuktasya yoginam*, constant engagement in yoga. In conclusion to chapter 8, Krishna says *yoga-yuktah*, be always fixed in devotion.

Chapter 9 opens with Krishna telling Arjuna that what he is teaching him now is 'the most confidential knowledge' and that by 'knowing which you shall be relieved of the miseries of material existence'. Through the chapter, he continues this theme of yoga being the path to attain the Supreme, even promising those who constantly worship him with love and devotion to 'carry what they lack' in their practice, *yoga-ksemam vahamy aham*, thus allowing the yoga practitioner to reach him. In chapter 9, verse 28, Krishna tells Arjuna again that by *yoga-yuktatma,* by being completely absorbed in him, Arjuna will reach him.

TRY THIS

So, we simply appreciate the life around us as a manifestation of the divine energy of the Supreme. We start to immediately respond to those things that occur or which exist around us as opportunities to meditate on the poetic and beautiful qualities of the Supreme. Then, we reach the stage of realization that this is truly the path of being 'relieved of the miseries of material existence'.

Krishna has said in chapter 2: 'One who is not connected with the Supreme can have neither transcendental intelligence nor a steady mind, without which there is no possibility of peace. And how can there be any happiness without peace?' Thus, to attain this state of being happy and peaceful, there are no tricks or money required; all one needs is the willingness to understand how we can actually transcend those issues and problems in life that so disturb us.

Yoga Means Using Our Highest Intelligence

In the second chapter of the Gita, and as mentioned in the previous section, Krishna talked of buddhi yoga and told Arjuna he would elaborate on the subject later. Now, in verse 10 of chapter 10, Krishna shows how buddhi yoga can achieve the highest goal of yoga: bhakti. In fact, verse 10 is at the heart of the Gita's four 'seed' verses. The seed verses (verses 8–11) are the essence of the Gita's teachings, and the key to bhakti yoga. These four seed verses are as follows:

aham sarvasya prabhavo
mattah sarvam pravartate
iti matva bhajante mam
budha bhava-samanvitah

'I am the source of all spiritual and material worlds. Everything emanates from Me. The wise who perfectly know this engage in My devotional service and worship Me with all their hearts.'

mac-citta mad-gata-prana
bodhayantah parasparam
kathayantas ca mam nityam
tusyanti ca ramanti ca

'The thoughts of My pure devotees dwell in Me, their lives are fully devoted to My service, and they derive great satisfaction and bliss from always enlightening one another and conversing about Me.'

tesam satata-yuktanam
bhajatam priti-purvakam
dadami buddhi-yogam tam
yena mam upayanti te

'To those who are constantly devoted to serving Me with love, I give the understanding by which they can come to Me.'

tesam evanukampartham
aham ajnana-jam tamah
nasayamy atma-bhava-stho
jnana-dipena bhasvata

'To show them special mercy, I, dwelling in their hearts, destroy with the shining lamp of knowledge the darkness born of ignorance.'

All four verses have a general meaning for yoga practitioners; they also have an esoteric meaning for those more advanced in bhakti yoga. But no matter how you approach these verses, they remain the essence of the teachings of the Bhagavad Gita. Why are these *catuh-sloki*, four verses, understood to be central to the Gita's teachings? There are two reasons for this: one, Krishna is the source of everything; two, bhakti yoga is the process by which to attain him.

It is Arjuna who speaks now, in verse 17, when he addresses Krishna as the 'yogi', the Supreme Mystic, and asks him how he is to think of him and know him. He seeks to know what Krishna's various forms are.

In response, Krishna recites his splendid attributes to Arjuna through an exceptionally beautiful series of verses in the Gita. He does say though that these are only a few of his 'splendorous manifestations', for his 'opulence is limitless'.

Of lights I am the radiant sun;
among the stars I am the moon;
of senses I am the mind;
of bodies of water I am the ocean;
of sacrifices I am the chanting of the holy names;
of immovable things I am the Himalayas;
among men I am the monarch;
among dispensers of law I am Yama, the Lord of Death;
among subduers I am time;
of flowing rivers I am the Ganges;
of all sciences I am the spiritual science of the self;
among logicians I am the conclusive truth;
among women I am fame, fortune, fine speech,
memory, intelligence, steadfastness, and patience;
of months I am November, and of seasons I am flower-bearing Spring;
I am also the gambling of cheats, and of the splendid I am the splendour;
I am victory, I am adventure, and I am the strength of the strong;
of those who seek victory I am morality;
of secret things I am silence, and of the wise I am the wisdom.[1]

These poetic verses are themselves a sadhana, a method of 'union with the Divine', by seeing all things in connection

[1] Bhaktivedanta Swami, *Bhagavad-gita As It Is,* Bhaktivedanta Book Trust, 1972.

with Krishna. As I have shared with you in the last few *Try this* summaries, it is important to train our thoughts to respond to everything around us, and this helps strengthen and expand our yoga practice. It would help if we did not react in extremes to situations, be it happiness or sadness or even heat or cold, but rather to see them simply as the workings of the world, and to maintain our calm and peace while things occur around us.

Thus, we learn that Krishna is in everything. All the things that surround us, that make up our days and our lives, all that we do, think and say, are *Krishna*. This meditative sadhana is part of our yoga practice. This section is a practical guide in learning how everything in creation is part of our yoga sadhana, and how we can respond to everything that exists – whether it appears as negative or positive – as being a part of the divine energy of the Lord. This is quite an advanced stage of sadhana. But it is important to understand that yogic sadhana is a process, where we will repeatedly stumble, fail, start again, fail again and move on yet again. It takes time, work and refinement, and the Gita is a step-by-step guide to help us attain this final spiritual goal.

TRY THIS

We now subtly shift gears in our daily yoga practice and move into the conscious meditation on the qualities of the Supreme as a means of nurturing the tender growth of the spiritual creeper in our hearts. This is both the core and the goal of our sadhana. Try it...

Yoga Means Everything in Creation is Krishna

In the opening verses of chapter 11, verses 1–3, Arjuna tells Krishna that as a result of his instruction and guidance, the grief and despair he was overwhelmed by have been dispelled.

Now, in verse 4, Arjuna addresses Krishna as Yogesvara – 'the master of all mystic power'.

manyase yadi tac chakyam
maya drastum iti prabho
yogesvara tato me tvam
darsayatmanam avyayam

Arjuna tells Krishna that if he thinks he is able, then to please reveal his cosmic form to Arjuna. Bhaktivedanta Swami writes in his commentary to these verses:

> This means that Arjuna no longer thinks of Krishna as a mere human being, as a friend of his, but as the source of everything. Arjuna is very enlightened and is glad that he has such a great friend as Krishna, but now he is

thinking that although he may accept Krishna as the source of everything, others may not. So in order to establish Krishna's divinity for all, he is requesting Krishna in this chapter to show His universal form.

In other words, Arjuna is asking Krishna to show, for the sake of everyone, that everything in creation is him, Krishna.

The name Yogesvara is repeated in verse 9 where Arjuna calls him Maha-yogesvara. Through this revelation of his universal form, Krishna is displaying his yogic potencies to Arjuna. He is, after all, the creator of yoga, and the Supreme Yogi!

Yoga Means Devotion

Chapter 12 is entitled 'Devotional Service', which is possibly the most direct and succinct English translation of 'bhakti yoga'. It is the shortest chapter of the Gita, with only 15 verses, but the majority of those verses refer specifically to bhakti yoga.

In verse 1, the word 'yoga' is spoken again by Arjuna when he asks Krishna, *ke yoga-vit-tamah,* who is the most perfect in knowledge of yoga? He asks Krishna whether it is the person who engages in bhakti yoga, or one who meditates on the unmanifest, the impersonal form of the Lord. In verse 2, Krishna answers by stating that it is those who fix their minds on his personal form and are always engaged in worshipping him with great transcendental faith who have achieved a level of perfection in their yoga practice.

In verses 6 and 7, Krishna elaborates with the words *ananyenaiva yogena*, without deviation, but it is from verse 9 that the beauty of chapter 12 reveals itself. Krishna opens the door to a spiritual yoga practice to all those who simply desire it. He does not limit it to just those who are already pure and qualified to attain the Supreme, or those who are expertly qualified in hatha or ashtanga yoga. Krishna says:

atha cittam samadhatum
na saknosi mayi sthiram
abhyasa-yogena tato
mam icchaptum dhananjaya

Bhaktivedanta Swami translates: 'If you are not able to fix your mind on me steadily, then by the practice of bhakti, devotional service, develop this desire.'

It is perhaps timely to note that this verse underscores Krishna's words to Arjuna in the first section of the Gita in terms of controlling the mind and senses. Krishna teaches that there are two types of yoga: one that comes spontaneously because the mind has been conquered; and the other which is based on endeavour or effort because the mind is still not fully controlled by the higher intelligence.

Up to this point in the Gita, Krishna has engaged in a lengthy and detailed discussion with Arjuna about how to overcome the problems of life; he has given step-by-step instructions on how to control the mind, turn to a higher intelligence, utilize one's innate intelligence, be conscious of the divine creation, meditate on the beautiful energy and characteristics of Krishna, and so on – all of which are summarized in the *Try this* sections.

In the next few verses, Krishna continues to break down the seemingly impossible heights of perfection required to attain him. Then, in verse 10, he says that if everything he has taught and all the discussions he has engaged in with Arjuna are not something that Arjuna can implement, then 'just work in consciousness of me'. He advises further, in verse 11: *asakto 'si kartum mad-yogam*, if you are unable to do this, then be self-situated, be content with your situation.

The teachings Krishna has been giving Arjuna are not easy, though they are simple. It does not mean that we should dismiss them because he says that if we can't do them, we can start with something easier. We need to follow the simple guidelines to understand, practise and attain the goal of yoga in the full sense. But, at the same time, Krishna recognizes that not everyone wants to be, or can be, a yogi. Further, not everyone has the same capacity, desire, karma, etc. Everyone is unique. Krishna has given a very detailed map by which we may charter our life's path and reach our highest potential, and that map is designed to guide everyone.

In verse 12, Krishna says that if these things are not possible, then one should cultivate knowledge. Better than knowledge is the practice of meditation. And better still is the renunciation of the fruits of one's actions, which gives peace of mind. Krishna is offering levels of bhakti yoga according to one's ability to commit, making it possible for everyone, at any stage of their yoga practice, to engage in devotional service, bhakti yoga.

And this is how we understand that the essence of yoga is bhakti, that the goal of yoga is bhakti, that the method is bhakti, and the supreme attainment is bhakti. This is yoga!

TRY THIS

Now that we've stepped into consciously meditating on the energies and qualities of the Supreme, we go further and enter the realm of consciously and actively engaging in bhakti yoga, which is a most crucial element in one's yoga practice. It is the key to selflessness, and transforms one's yoga practice into a rich and deep sadhana.

In the concluding verses of chapter 12, Krishna describes how, when one is trying, or even desiring to try to practise bhakti yoga, that person is very dear to him. In verse 14, he speaks of the qualities that endear a person to him:

santustah satatam yogi
yatatma drdha-niscayah
mayy arpita-mano-buddhir
yo mad-bhaktah sa me priyah

This is a beautiful, embracing verse. Krishna is simply stating what qualities in a person appeal to him: one who is not envious, who is kind to all, free from ego, equal in both happiness and distress. And one who is engaged in devotion, *santusta satatam yogi*, is always satisfied. And, if one is very dear to Krishna, he or she has achieved the goal of yoga.

And that is 'yoga' in chapters 6–12 of the Bhagavad Gita. The difference between the first six chapters and the next six is a marked one: in the first section, Krishna is gently introducing Arjuna to the understanding of what causes his confusion, distress, illusion and fear; he offers explanations to bring him out of the 'forest of delusion' and guides him through myriad subject matters such as the nature of the soul, the workings of the mind, the power of the senses and how to control them, the effect the senses have on a person, the basics of yoga, the practice of yoga and the intelligence. In the second section, when Arjuna is ready to hear the direct, absolute solution to life's problems, then we learn how yoga means connecting with Krishna, the Supreme Lord, and how to absorb one's mind, intelligence and practices in him; we learn that yoga destroys the miseries of life and that at the end of life, absorbed in yoga, one attains him.

Despite the depths and heights of this division of the Gita, 'yoga' is mentioned far less in these chapters than it is in the first division of chapters. Those chapters were the preparation, while these are the heart.

Now, let us summarize what we have learnt so far:

1. We learn to see those things around us – nature, life, family – as opportunities to appreciate the qualities of the Supreme Lord.
2. By doing so, we strengthen and deepen our daily yoga practice. Thus, our reactions and responses to things that happen in life are honed, refined and softened.
3. In reaching this level, we fix our meditation to a set 'speed' in the background of our daily lives, strengthening the core of our yoga practice.
4. By establishing this foundation of training the mind and senses towards certain aspects of the Divine Nature, we now begin our practice of consciously meditating on the beauty and opulence of the Supreme – the qualities that Krishna describes to Arjuna.
5. From this strong core of a conscious yoga practice comes the next stage of our spiritual depth in yoga: the realm of actively and consciously engaging in bhakti yoga, devotional service.
6. Finally, as we start to nurture a rich and deep spiritual sadhana, we become aware of those qualities within ourselves that will either help us in our yoga practice or create obstacles. When we meditate on the opulence and beauty of the Divine, simultaneously being conscious of the positive qualities in ourselves we see rising through our sadhana, we firmly establish in ourselves a strong spiritual core.

CHAPTER 3

The Perfection of Knowledge

THE SUBJECT OF THESE six chapters is jnana yoga, the yoga of knowledge. Without application, the value of knowledge is limited. Einstein acknowledged that 'wisdom is not a product of schooling but of the lifelong attempt to acquire it'. The application of knowledge is a key subject in the Gita.

The chapters on bhakti yoga precede those on jnana yoga for a reason. There is a profound logic to the order in which Krishna teaches Arjuna, which was explained at the beginning of this book: the first six chapters are on karma yoga, the subsequent six chapters are on bhakti yoga, and the final six are on jnana yoga.

In this third and final section of the Gita, from chapters 13 to 18, Krishna goes into specific detail on how a human being functions under the influence of material and spiritual energies, and the qualities of a person who is situated in the higher and lower states of consciousness. He also elaborates on the three modes of material nature. In doing so, he specifically addresses how one avoids distress, anxiety, sadness and other negative emotions, and how, 'armed with yoga', one can actually overcome the obstacles of daily life.

Yoga Means that 'High Quality' Becomes Our Nature

In verses 8–12 of chapter 13, Krishna gives an eloquent oration of high qualities, wherein yoga and bhakti are both mentioned. These five verses form a sound meditation for us on what our inner yoga sadhana should look like, and what qualities we are trying to prioritize in order to strengthen our yoga practice:

amanitvam adambhitvam
ahimsa ksantir arjavam
acaryopasanam saucam
sthairyam atma-vinigrahah

indriyarthesu vairagyam
anahankara eva ca
janma-mrtyu-jara-vyadhi-
duhkha-dosanudarsanam

asaktir anabhisvangah
putra-dara-grhadisu
nityam ca sama-cittatvam
istanistopapattisu

mayi cananya-yogena
bhaktir avyabhicarini
vivikta-desa-sevitvam
aratir jana-samsadi

I will let Bhaktivedanta Swami translate this: 'Humility; pridelessness; non-violence; tolerance; simplicity; approaching a bona fide spiritual master; cleanliness; steadiness; self-control; renunciation of the objects of sense gratification; absence of false ego; the perception of the evil of birth, death, old age and disease; detachment; freedom from entanglement with children, wife, home and the rest; even-mindedness amid pleasant and unpleasant events; constant and unalloyed devotion to Me; aspiring to live in a solitary place; detachment from the general mass of people; accepting the importance of self-realization; and philosophical search for the Absolute Truth – all these I declare to be knowledge, and besides this whatever there may be is ignorance.'

As we will see in the coming pages, these qualities that Krishna speaks of are similar to Patanjali's yamas – ethical disciplines – and niyamas – rules of conduct. There are distinct parallels between Krishna's teachings on what forms the foundational character of a yoga practitioner and Patanjali's teachings, which are an elaborate and detailed expansion on the study of these qualities as given in the Gita.

Yoga Means Meditation, Philosophy and Action

In the early verses of chapter 13, Krishna introduces and goes into specific detail about the Supreme Soul, the Lord within the heart or, as Krishna calls himself, the Supersoul.

In verse 25, Krishna explains how one can know the Divine through three different ways. One way is through dhyana yoga – meditation; another is through sankhya yoga – philosophy; and the third is through karma yoga – work or actions. Krishna is conveying that while there are various paths that one can take to achieve the goal in yoga, all paths lead to one place, despite how different they may appear.

dhyanenatmani pasyanti
kecid atmanam atmana
anye sankhyena yogena
karma-yogena capare

Yoga Means Knowledge

We have already explained earlier in this book how yoga means knowledge. In chapter 4, Krishna teaches that the knowledge of how to control the mind, senses and intelligence can take one beyond misery and suffering, and open the door to a more mature experience of one's yoga practice. But in chapter 14, we are given a deeper philosophical discourse on how 'yoga means knowledge' – the knowledge of nature, those who live in the world, and their consciousness.

The word 'yoga' is only mentioned in the concluding verses of chapter 14 when Krishna uses the term *bhakti-yogena* which, as you know by now, means yoga in action, or practising devotional service: 'One who engages in full devotional service, unfailing in all circumstances, at once transcends the modes of material nature.'

mam ca yo 'vyabhicarena
bhakti-yogena sevate
sa gunan samatityaitan
brahma-bhuyaya kalpate

In other words, although the entire chapter is expounding philosophy, it concludes with the understanding given in the previous chapters: bhakti yoga is the goal of this knowledge.

Similarly, chapter 15 begins by explaining the process of breaking one's attachment to the material world. Krishna speaks of this in verse 9, where he says that despite the profundity of these subject matters, one whose eyes are trained in knowledge can see or understand this wisdom.

The word 'yoga' arises in verse 11, when Krishna speaks of how one must endeavour, comparing the results of such endeavours with those who do not endeavour:

yatanto yoginas cainam
pasyanty atmany avasthitam
yatanto 'py akrtatmano
nainam pasyanty acetasah

'The endeavouring transcendentalists who are situated in self-realization can see all this clearly. But those whose minds are not developed and who are not situated in self-realization cannot see what is taking place, though they may try to.'

TRY THIS

Look back over the 'Try this' entries as summarized at the end of each section, and see how you are progressing in your yoga practice.

Krishna has repeated that raising oneself to the level of being fixed in meditation is only possible through the steady control of the mind and senses, and directing them towards one's own paths of thought: the mind is not in control, but one's own good qualities must be brought to the fore as the lesser qualities are diminished – all these things are the beginning of the process of self-realization.

Yoga Means Surrender

The word 'yoga' appears in the title of chapter 15, 'The Yoga of the Supreme person'. Naturally, in a book that discusses the source of yoga and many uses of this word, we would be remiss in passing by this title.

The main topic of chapter 15 is surrender. Krishna also practises surrender, and that is what the title of this chapter actually means. He surrenders to his devotee, reciprocating that surrender. To Arjuna, he is surrendered in service, becoming his chariot driver. In this way, Krishna is also experiencing and relishing the practice of yoga, because the surrendering process in yoga is what gives it its taste.

Although this may be an esoteric topic, it is at the same time quite simple: through the experiencing of the yoga process – from its beginning stages in the early chapters of the Gita, up to these current chapters, we develop a higher consciousness. In chapter 13, verses 8–12, the qualities Krishna speaks of include humility, and one does not acquire humility without surrendering the ego and the mind (please refer to page 74 for the full list of qualities as given by Bhaktivedanta Swami). Surrender becomes part of our practice and, at the same time, higher qualities blossom within us; their presence is the satisfying 'flavour' of yoga.

Yoga Means Divine Qualities

I've mentioned earlier how some words these days become overused, ordinary even, despite their source being far from ordinary, for example, words like 'spiritual' or 'divine'. But we can note as we make our way through the Gita how the word 'divine' is very specific. The dictionary definition of this word is 'of or like God'. In other words, anything that is actually 'divine' has its source in, or actually is, God.

In chapter 16, Krishna elaborates on the qualities that are acquired by those practising bhakti yoga (verses 1–3). Those who practise bhakti yoga become endowed with a 'divine nature'. As with the oration of qualities in chapter 13, these qualities also parallel Patanjali's yamas and niyamas and specifically mention his fourth niyama, *svadhyayah*, studying the self and scripture. These are beautiful verses and their translation is worth meditating on here: 'Fearlessness; purification of one's existence; cultivation of spiritual knowledge; charity; self-control; performance of sacrifice; study of the Vedas; austerity; simplicity; non-violence; truthfulness; freedom from anger; renunciation; tranquillity; aversion to fault-finding; compassion for all living entities; freedom from covetousness; gentleness; modesty; steady determination; vigour; forgiveness; fortitude; cleanliness; and freedom from envy and from the passion for honour – these transcendental qualities, O son of Bharata, belong to godly men endowed with divine nature.'

It is also significant to note that knowledge is emphasized once again: Krishna uses the term *jnana-yoga-vyavasthitih*, that one must be situated in knowledge. Back in chapter 4 of the Gita, Krishna tells Arjuna that when one acts upon this knowledge, he experiences the 'mature fruit' of that knowledge. And the 'mature fruit' is revealed here: it is the development of divine qualities.

TRY THIS

Our yoga practice is a constant process of checking in with ourselves: we should always go back to where we began and observe our progress through the different branches of knowledge we are reading and absorbing. Therefore, at this point, I'm going to list the 'Try this' summaries from the earlier parts of this book. Do read them through and see how your mind and consciousness have changed since you began this practical and applicable process of yoga:

1. *Don't lose your intelligence or let it be overwhelmed by the mind and emotions.*
2. *Ask someone wise, senior or more qualified for guidance, or think of what they would do in your situation.*
3. *'Act in yoga'. Make that call, connect yourself to the Lord through prayer or meditation. The outcome is guaranteed.*
4. *Every morning, think of this phrase: 'armed with yoga'.*
5. *Don't react, don't rely on your external 'crutches' to get you through what arises: just pause, think of the practical steps given to Arjuna by Krishna, and flow.*
6. *Learn to see the things around you – nature, life, family – as opportunities to appreciate the qualities of the Supreme Lord. By doing so, you strengthen and deepen your daily yoga practice. As a result, your responses to things that happen in life will become refined.*
7. *Your meditation is adjusted to a set speed in the*

background of your daily life, strengthening the core of your yoga practice.

8. *By establishing this foundation of training the mind and senses towards certain aspects of the Divine Nature, you now begin your practice of consciously meditating on the beauty and opulence of the Supreme.*
9. *From this strong core of a conscious yoga practice comes the next stage: the realm of actively and consciously engaging in bhakti yoga.*
10. *Finally, as you start to nurture your sadhana, you become conscious of those qualities within yourself that will either help you in your yoga practice, or create obstacles for you. When you meditate on the opulence and beauty of the Divine, simultaneously being conscious of the positive qualities in yourself you see arising through your practice, you firmly establish within a strong spiritual core for your yoga practice.*

As I have mentioned earlier, it is important to note that while the word 'yoga' may not be specifically mentioned, the opposite of what yoga is, is often mentioned, giving the dual understanding of what it is and what it is not. Every verse in the Gita is about yoga as you understand by now.

Thus, in chapter 16, while being given detailed information about one endowed with a divine nature, we are also given detailed information about the absolute opposite:

a nature that has evil or demonic qualities. While we can list the divine qualities and track our own progress to see how we have developed higher qualities, it is also worthwhile to check for our lower qualities, to see how we have managed to control, change or remove them from our conditioned thoughts and actions. Krishna speaks of these lower qualities to Arjuna, and perhaps the most significant thing to note is how brief the list is compared to the oration of higher qualities. Krishna says quite succinctly: 'Pride, arrogance, conceit, anger, harshness and ignorance – these qualities belong to those of demonic nature' (16.4).

Yoga Means Faith

'Yoga means faith' is an interesting title. I have written earlier in the book that yoga is not a faith or belief system; nor is it a religion. Instead, it is a science and a practice. So how does yoga mean faith?

While chapter 17 does not mention the word yoga, it is nonetheless a direct thesis on faith. In particular, this chapter details how one acquires faith, what form that faith takes, how faith is dependent on one's consciousness and habits, and how much one is able to control the mind and senses.

According to the Gita, the modes or characteristics of material nature are divided into three categories: goodness, passion and ignorance. Everything in the material world falls into one of these categories, including a person's nature, actions, thoughts, speech, moods and qualities. Everything we are and do is included here. In fact, we are born in a particular mode. India is one of the very few countries whose inhabitants, across the board, are interested in the hour and day of birth, what planet is ruling when one is born, and what things lie in the future according to the time, place and situation of one's birth. Everyone rushes to have the astrological chart created for a newborn in the family, to see what auspicious (and inauspicious) things might befall this new arrival, what the baby's nature will be, and what qualities they will possess. This is a deep and fascinating science, and while it is explained clearly in the Gita in chapter 14, it is mentioned throughout the Gita and most specifically here in chapter 17, in terms of faith.

But one thing should be very clear: while knowledge about these modes of nature – goodness, passion, ignorance – and how they determine our character, nature and qualities, informs us, this information need not actually *define* us. For example, those born in unfortunate circumstances do not necessarily have an unfortunate life: they can be happy, satisfied, humble, accepting and filled with divine qualities. On the other hand, those who are rich, famous, beautiful or intelligent are not automatically endowed with divine qualities, spiritual intelligence or advanced yoga abilities. No matter who one is and where and to whom one is born, one can choose to use one's life as an impetus to elevate oneself in yoga and to cultivate and nurture one's innate divine qualities. Or, one can allow oneself to be overwhelmed by the mode under which one was born, and to be ruled by material nature, be a 'victim' of circumstance. It's always our own choice.

And the divisions of faith, as Krishna points out in this chapter of the Gita, are ruled by those same modes that we are: the modes of goodness, passion and ignorance. Even more specifically, our own faith is decided by which mode we allow ourselves to be ruled by. That is to say, if we allow ourselves to be controlled by the obstacles in life that assail us, or difficulties that we come face to face with, then our faith will also be ruled by ignorance or passion and not goodness.

By reading and understanding these chapters and being *jnana-yoga-vyavasthiti*, firmly situated in knowledge (as Krishna spoke of in chapter 16, verse 1), we can easily identify what is conducive to our yoga practice and what is not; what elevates us spiritually and what does not; what causes misery, depression, anxiety, lamentation, moroseness, fear, confusion and sadness, and what results in happiness, freedom from anxiety, peace and other 'positive' emotions. While the lower modes of nature, or things in the mode of ignorance can strike us at any time – and often do so on a daily basis – knowledge of yoga gives us the understanding by which we can deal with and overcome distressing or upsetting situations.

Consequently, these chapters are a crucial ingredient not only in the practice of yoga but also in the understanding of life itself. The Gita helps us understand how to extract ourselves from negative situations, and how to elevate the self – the mind and consciousness, to a 'higher ground'. As Krishna says in verse 58 of chapter 18, 'If you become conscious of Me, you will pass over all the obstacles of conditioned life by My grace. If, however, you do not work in such consciousness but act through false ego, not hearing Me, you will be lost.'

TRY THIS

Read through chapter 17 in the Gita, focusing on yourself and your qualities, both negative and positive, divine and demonic. Consider with your new mindset, with the knowledge you have acquired so far by reading through Krishna's talks with Arjuna, how much you have adjusted your consciousness already, how new, previously unseen qualities are surfacing in you, and how other less beneficial characteristics are becoming less and less apparent as you progress through your yoga practice.

Yoga Means Elevation to a Higher Consciousness

The majority of verses in this final chapter are a continuation of chapter 17, and are what can be called 'comparative verses', where one can compare the results of actions performed or problems faced in the mode of goodness with actions that take place in the mode of passion or ignorance.

dhrtya yaya dharayate
manahs-pranendriya-kriyah
yogenavyabhicarinya
dhrtih sa partha sattviki

Krishna explains the mode of goodness to Arjuna, telling him that when a person displays unbreakable determination, and when they maintain that determination through the practice of yoga, they are simultaneously controlling the mind and senses, and this is a direct definition of the mode of goodness.

Throughout this section (chapters 13–18), we have learned the varied sciences of nature, the nature of the self as well as of the Supreme, the nature of material energy, and how to live according to the nature we ourselves are born with. Now Krishna is preparing Arjuna for the ultimate knowledge, and the last verses of the Gita focus on this subject.

At some point or the other in this book, you may have wondered if this information is all too much, if self-realization is possible to attain, if it really works, if you're on the right path, doing the right thing, reading the right material. Well, Krishna addresses this in verse 37 when he speaks of intelligence, and says to Arjuna, 'That which in the beginning may be just like poison but at the end is just like nectar and which awakens one to self-realization is said to be happiness in the mode of goodness.'

It may be difficult to take something up, to struggle to establish it as an ongoing practice in our lives and keep at it until we actually see some result. But Krishna acknowledges that things are often like 'poison in the beginning but nectar in the end'. In the commentary to this verse, Bhaktivedanta Swami writes, 'In the pursuit of self-realization, one has to follow many rules and regulations to control the mind and the senses and to concentrate the mind on the self. All these procedures are very difficult, bitter like poison, but if one is successful in following the regulations and comes to the transcendental position, he begins to drink real nectar, and he enjoys life.'

As I've said earlier, the Gita's teachings are simple, though not easy. However, by following the step-by-step guidelines that take us progressively through this book and through the Gita, we can 'enjoy life'.

Patanjali points out in the *Yoga Sutras* that the higher stages of yoga cannot be entered into with intellect, for they require a mature practice and a wisdom acquired from the knowledge and realization of life, the self and the world. In verse 55, Krishna says the same things using the word 'bhakti'.

bhaktya mam abhijanati
yavan yas casmi tattvatah
tato mam tattvato jnatva
visate tad-anantaram

'One can understand Me as I am, as the Supreme Personality of Godhead, only by devotional service. And when one is in full consciousness of Me by such devotion, he can enter into the kingdom of God.'

And, even more interestingly, Krishna says that it is buddhi yoga, using the intelligence, that will give one the qualification to attain this level:

cetasa sarva-karmani
mayi sannyasya mat-parah
buddhi-yogam upasritya
mac-cittah satatam bhava

'In all activities just depend upon Me and work always under My protection. With the intelligence thus guided by devotion, be fully conscious of Me.'

It has been mentioned earlier that the mind and senses are controlled by the intelligence and that intelligence, in turn, is controlled by the soul. Krishna states this clearly in this verse by saying that 'with the intelligence thus guided by devotion', one can be fully conscious of him.

However, the most interesting conclusion to all that has been taught so far in the Gita is now presented by Krishna, when he says in chapter 18, verse 63, 'Thus, I have explained to you knowledge still more confidential. Deliberate on this fully, and then do what you wish to do.'

Previously, at the end of the second division of the Gita (chapters 7–12), Krishna makes a similar point. He says that bhakti is entirely dependent on the desire and level of surrender of the individual; it is not dependent on the foundations of any yoga practice or philosophy. 'Do what you wish to do' is hardly what one would expect to read in such a text, but this is the nature of bhakti and the key to one's success or failure, happiness or distress, misery or freedom from trouble. Free will is paramount: we *choose* what to do in any particular situation. For example, we choose to allow ourselves to be overwhelmed or to put into practice the wisdom we have acquired, and rise above the challenges that affect us.

The final section of this book is entitled 'Entering an Internal Practice: The Last Six Limbs of Yoga', where Patanjali instructs that we must go beyond the mind, senses and intellect, and enter into a deeper yoga practice. Now, in this section of the Gita, Krishna is similarly taking Arjuna to that next step: he asks Arjuna in chapter 18, verse 72, 'Are your illusions now dispelled?' The answer is yes, because Arjuna has heard a discourse on life, suffering and knowledge, on devotion and higher qualities, on how to raise the self up from depression, anger, fear and other negative states. And Arjuna has heard all of this from the *param yogam yogesvara*, the supreme mystic yogi, Krishna. Verse 78 concludes with these words: 'Wherever there is Krishna, the master of all mystics, and wherever there is Arjuna, the supreme archer, there will also certainly be opulence, victory, extraordinary power and morality.'

TRY THIS

Again, let's meditate on what we've learned and summarize our learning into brief points that encapsulate the deep and extensive teachings Krishna is imparting to Arjuna:

1. *As you know by now, 'yoga' means to link or connect with the Supreme. 'One who is not connected with the Supreme can have neither transcendental intelligence nor a steady mind, without which there is no possibility of peace. And how can there be any happiness without peace?' Thus, we start to recognize our internal yoga practice developing.*
2. *We prepare for the next stages of our yoga practice by acquiring the knowledge of what lies ahead. In the forthcoming section of the book, you will be introduced to the yamas and niyamas. Knowing these qualities is crucial in solidifying the core of one's yoga practice. Through the unfolding essence of Patanjali's foundational principles, you will be encouraged to do a daily exercise where you focus on one of them, strengthening the previously-learned tip of actively and consciously developing your inner qualities.*
3. *This section has focused on reviewing the progress of one's mind and senses as well as the development of one's inner qualities. We can see how the acquiring and steady refining of those inner qualities simultaneously accomplishes the control of the mind and senses, for the two are not separate.*

4. *In a previous 'Try this' summary, we learned that there is no such thing as failure. Through the continual process of checking in with oneself that this section has invited us to do, we start to see this concept of 'no such thing as failure' as we progress in our yoga practice, even if only with the tiniest of steps!*

CHAPTER 4

Sadhana: The Basis and Sustainer of Yoga

SO FAR, WE HAVE discussed the many meanings of yoga through the chapters of the Bhagavad Gita. An obvious omission to the experienced practitioner's eye is the very core of the word 'practitioner', which is 'practice'.

Yoga is a practice, and through the three sections of the Gita, Krishna has consistently explained the progressive stages of sadhana and the practice of yoga. Yogacharya B.K.S. Iyengar uses the term 'sadhana' consistently in his writings, and chapter 2 of Patanjali's *Yoga Sutras* is entitled 'Sadhana-pada', which details what is required to take the sadhaka, the practitioner, to the higher, internal levels of yoga.

The word 'sadhana' is deep in its meaning and purpose. In the *Yoga Sutras*, Patanjali writes in detail of the effect of yoga, and what impact one's yoga sadhana has on the consciousness, emotions, intellect, physiognomy and even on the soul and the innermost chambers of the heart. In the same way, Krishna speaks to Arjuna of the progressive stages of yoga, the nature of the soul, freedom from miseries and distress, the Supersoul – the Divine Soul of the Lord present within the heart of every living being – and the realizations one achieves on these subjects from one's own sadhana.

When speaking of yoga, the word 'practice' is used more often than 'sadhana.' Practice can also mean that simply by repeated action one can achieve an advanced stage of yoga. While one may certainly make some progress physically on the yogic path, mere exercise does not incorporate the deeper, more internal elements of yoga. 'Sadhana', therefore, is used to encompass both the physical and internal aspects of yoga.

This understanding of sadhana is required before moving on to yamas and niyamas. The work on the self that one's sadhana involves is essential to grasp the true significance of yamas and niyamas. Sadhana, therefore, serves as both the foundation of one's yoga and as the means to acquire the deeper, internal stages that Patanjali refers to, and which I expand upon in the final section of this book.

Therefore, the Bhagavad Gita and the *Yoga Sutras* parallel each other's teachings on the practice of yoga and the progressive depth and advancement one makes according to one's level of commitment.

PART 2

YAMAS AND NIYAMAS

The Foundations of Yoga

CHAPTER 1

The Yogic Systems

BEFORE WE DELVE INTO the different limbs of Patanjali's yoga, with its various sub-categories, let us look at the different kinds of yogic systems that exist.

ASHTANGA YOGA

'Asta' means eight and 'anga' refers to limbs. Created by the sage Patanjali and detailed in his *Yoga Sutras*, ashtanga yoga is a system of yoga that focuses on eight specific limbs or categories, which are as follows:

Yama

The first limb, yama, is best described as the ethical discipline of one's yoga practice. It looks at behaviour and how one should conduct oneself, and asks one to adhere to universally accepted standards of good behavior. There are five yamas:

- *Ahimsa*, non-violence
- *Satya*, truth

- *Asteya*, integrity
- *Brahmacharya*, abstinence or restraint
- *Aparigraha*, non-possessiveness

Niyama

Niyama, the second limb, looks at the rules of conduct of a yoga practitioner. These are the 'dos' of yoga, which we actively carry out to enhance our character and yoga practice; for example, developing an attitude of humility, compassion, kindness and awareness through spiritual customs like visiting a temple, mosque or church to offer prayers. The five niyamas are as follows:

- *Saucham*, purity
- *Santosh*, contentment
- *Tapas*, austerity
- *Svadhyaya*, study of the self and the scriptures
- *Ishvara-pranidhana*, meditation on the Supreme

Asana

Asana, or the postures done in yoga, comprises the third limb of ashtanga yoga. The practise of asana creates in the yoga practitioner an ability to be disciplined in mind and body, both of which are necessary for the higher yogic stages.

Pranayama

This fourth limb is composed from two Sanskrit words: 'prana', life force or the breath; and 'ayama', restraint or control. It refers to the art of breath that positively affects the psychological and physical health of a person. It rejuvenates the body and purifies the mind.

Pratyahara

Patanjali describes the fifth limb, pratyahara, as the bridge that takes the yoga practitioner from the external to the internal meditations of yoga – a transitional stage that leads the practitioner from conscious learning and practice into the more internal, 'unthinking' level of yoga sadhana. The word 'pratyahara' means withdrawing the mind and senses from external objects, a conscious closing of the mind to the pull of external energy. This is the stage of yoga practice where one is is not controlled any futher by the mind and senses.

Dharana

This sixth limb means concentration and introspective focus. It is a harnessing of all that we have gained control of and conquered within, and a conscious focusing on the next limb.

Dhyana

Dhyana is the uninterrupted flow of concentration. Although concentration (dharana) and meditation (dhyana) appear to be similar, there is a fine yet distinct line that separates them. Where dharana requires one-pointed attention, dhyana is contemplative and reflective, like a river: a stream of continuous thought, a current of contemplation, a flow of awareness and consciousness.

Samadhi

Patanjali describes this eighth and final stage of ashtanga yoga, samadhi, as a state of ecstasy. At this stage, the yoga practitioner realizes a profound union with the Divine. The Vedic dictionary, *Nirukti*, says, *samyag adhiyate 'sminn atma-tattva-yathatmyam*: 'When the mind is fixed for understanding the self, it is said to be in samadhi'. Samadhi is, in short, the ultimate goal of one's yoga sadhana.

BAHIRANGA

The first four limbs of Patanjali's eightfold system – yama, niyama, asana and pranayama – are collated into a category known as bahiranga. This system concentrates on refining the personality, gaining mastery over the body and developing an understanding of the self, all of which prepare one for the second half of this journey, which deals with the mind and senses.

ANTARANGA

The last four limbs of Patanjali's system – pratyahara, dharana, dhyana and samadhi – are also clubbed together into a category known as antaranga, which concentrates on the aspects of yoga that lead to a higher, more internal practice of yoga.

HATHA YOGA

While hatha yoga is a collection of yoga asanas and breath control, such as sitting poses, standing poses and breathing exercises, its emphasis is on the actual execution of the asanas.

The word 'hatha' itself means two complementary forces working together, 'ha' and 'tha'. In other words, in the physical practice of yoga, a teacher might say 'extend from the inner thigh to the inner ankle'. Here, the complementary but opposing energy is also present, for one also extends from the outer ankle to the outer thigh, thereby performing opposing but complementary actions. In this way, hatha yoga is present in the practice of yoga of any practitioner.

The difference between hatha yoga, Patanjali's ashtanga yoga and Krishna's teachings of yoga in the Gita is that Patanjali and Krishna focus on the yoga of the mind, senses and spirit, while hatha yoga works with the body and health. However, the *Yogatattva Upanishad*[1] does not recognize or acknowledge this distinction, and teaches a

---

[1] The Yogatattva Upanishad is a minor Upanishad, and a part of the *Krishna Yajurveda*. Yogatattva Upanishad is notable for presenting and explaining yoga in the Vaishnava tradition.

system that includes the entirety of Patanjali's teachings and all the additional elements of hatha yoga. For the sake of this handbook, we will refer only to ashtanga yoga and bhakti yoga.

CHAPTER 2

Yamas and Niyamas

THE YAMAS AND NIYAMAS are the foundational principles of yoga and make up the first two limbs of Patanjali's eightfold process of ashtanga yoga. These are guidelines: yamas are things one should not do, while niyamas are things one should do. They are, together, the ethical disciplines (yamas) and the moral code of conduct (niyamas) for yoga practitioners.

It is a globally recognized fact that Patanjali, the author of the *Yoga Sutras,* is the father of yoga. While not much is known about the sage Patanjali or his famous text, it is believed that he wrote the 196 sutras that make up the entirety of the *Yoga Sutras*, around 250 BCE. (It should be noted here that the *Mahabhasya,* the classic text on Sanskrit grammar, was not authored by the same Patanjali.)

Western education and history both place a lot of emphasis on knowing all the details of an author and their qualifications. Eastern philosophy, however, has a different perspective: the author often acts as a channel or a conduit for the higher knowledge and wisdom that is revealed through him or her, and in turn passes it on to those who seek knowledge of that particular subject. While Western educational methodology may have trouble assimilating this kind of approach, the East does not.

So what are these principles of yoga, and why did Patanjali consider them the necessary foundation upon which to build our yoga practice?

The yamas and niyamas are most often referred to as the dos and don'ts of human behaviour. But in terms of these first two limbs of ashtanga yoga, we need to reverse their application: the yamas are actually the don'ts, and the niyamas are the dos.

The direct translation of the word yama is 'restraint', and the five principles of the yamas encompass those things we should not do, for example, we should not lie, cheat, steal or be violent. Niyamas, on the other hand, encourage the things we should do, for instance, be pure, content, simple and godly…

As mentioned a little earlier, the yamas are as follows:

- *Ahimsa*, non-violence
- *Satya*, truth
- *Asteya*, integrity
- *Brahmacharya*, abstinence/restraint
- *Aparigraha*, non-possessiveness

The niyamas are as follows:

- *Saucham*, purity

- *Santosh*, contentment
- *Tapas*, austerity
- *Svadhyaya*, study of the scriptures in the matter of self-realization
- *Ishvara-pranidhana*, meditation on the Supreme

As to the benefits of observing and practising the yamas and niyamas, Yogacharya B.K.S. Iyengar says, 'Without a firm foundation, a house cannot stand. Without the practice of the principles of yama and niyama, which lay the foundation for building character, there cannot be an integrated personality. The practice of yoga without yama and niyama is mere acrobatics.'[1]

Krishna's talks with Arjuna in the Gita encompass all the elements of our progress through the yamas and niyamas in a practical and constructive way that embodies not only the practice of ashtanga yoga, but a deeper and more substantial understanding of how the universe works and our place in it. Patanjali takes these elements and expands upon them, creating a conscious and practical basis for anyone taking up yoga in any form.

The *Yoga Sutras* encompass the entirety of yoga's philosophy and practice, and while much can be written and said about the text that is considered the practical guide to yoga, only summarized studies into each of the eight limbs will be covered here. However, for a basic and lucid

---

[1] B.K.S. Iyengar, *Light on Yoga*, Unwin Hyman, 1989.

explanation on all 196 sutras, there are two books that lead the field and provide an easy dissemination of Patanjali's deep wisdom: B.K.S. Iyengar's *Light on the Yoga Sutras*[2] and Edwin Bryant's *The Yoga Sutras of Patanjali*.[3]

---

[2] B.K.S. Iyengar, *Light on the Yoga Sutras*, Thorsons, 1996.

[3] Edwin Bryant, *The Yoga Sutras of Patanjali, A New Edition, Translation and Commentary*, Northpoint Press, 2009.

CHAPTER 3

Ahimsa

Non-violence

Learning how not to arrest the progressive life of any living entity

WHILE THE DEFINITION OR translation of each yama or niyama can be just one or two words, the full character of the principle is like a many-branched tree, its delicate leaves spreading throughout all aspects of our being, and then beyond ourselves and our yoga practice into our relations with others, human and beast alike. With the first yama of ahimsa, non-violence, we will look at how it means so much more than just abstaining from violence, for the principle includes other behavioural aspects like speech, gesture, thought, consciousness and action.

In his commentary to Krishna's words on ahimsa, Bhaktivedanta Swami gives what is perhaps the most eloquent description of ahimsa that one is ever likely to find: 'Ahimsa means not arresting the progressive life of any living entity.'

What a wonderfully poetic and perfect phrase this is: 'not arresting the progressive life of any living entity'. But what does it really mean? When we speak of ahimsa, we immediately think of non-violent acts, like not killing. Perhaps a practical and relatable example of this is in the killing of animals simply to fill the stomach and gratify the senses. If one indeed believes in and claims to live the higher human principles of non-violence and compassion, then these values should naturally extend beyond ourselves to other creatures who are subject to our mercy and behaviour.

Vegetarianism has been a popular topic in matters of health, yoga, consciousness and spirituality in the twenty-first century, and now we also have its younger cousin, veganism. The fundamental philosophy of both vegetarianism and veganism is non-violence.

Looking at ahimsa in an expansive way, the topic is intensified in the Gita, with Krishna pushing Arjuna to fight; he even drives Arjuna's chariot right into the heart of the battle. And they face an opposing army who can't wait to commit acts of violence. Yet, the Gita's battlefield scenario is our reality check on what 'ahimsa' means in all its forms and aspects.

Krishna says to Arjuna in chapter 4: 'Therefore, the doubts which have arisen in your heart out of ignorance should be slashed by the weapon of knowledge. Armed with yoga, stand and fight.'

On the surface, it looks like Arjuna is the one wanting to observe ahimsa. He doesn't want to fight and doesn't see the point; he doesn't want to kill his relatives, teachers and his revered sagely grandfather, Bhishma. On the other hand, Krishna appears to use words that have a violent connotation. Yet the message here is a deeply spiritual one.

'Armed with yoga' means controlling the mind instead of being controlled by the mind, senses and emotions, and the subsequent feelings such things result in, like depression, despondency and confusion. 'Stand and fight', while perhaps a direct instruction in the moment, on the battlefield, is also a broader and more general indication of how we need to 'fight' negative obstacles in life. This is to be done with the teachings of yoga that Krishna is giving Arjuna.

When using the words 'armed' and 'fight', Krishna is talking about slashing ignorance to pieces with the weapon of knowledge, with the wisdom of yoga. The real battlefield is the self, and all the obstacles that the mind and the heart set before us.

As we have already learnt in the first section of the book, yoga means intelligence in action, a balanced mind and equilibrium. While 'stand and fight' may sound like an act of violence, the opposite is actually true: to destroy ignorance and to act in knowledge is, in fact, the most non-violent behaviour possible.

Yoga replaces our conditioned understanding of words and phrases with deeper knowledge and awareness.

There are other ways to 'arrest the progressive life', which don't involve a literal killing. To remain in ignorance is also an act of violence. Krishna knows that allowing ignorance to fester within oneself or in another *is* an act of violence as it arrests the spiritual development – indeed, the basic human evolvement, of a person. It is harm that Arjuna seems intent on inflicting upon himself. Thus, Krishna attacks Arjuna's ignorance with the sword of knowledge.

In chapter 10, verse 11, Krishna says to Arjuna, 'I destroy with the shining lamp of knowledge the darkness born of ignorance.' This 'shining light of knowledge' is represented by the qualities Krishna lists in chapter 13, verses 8–11 – qualities that include the ahimsa we are speaking of now (please refer to page 74 for a full list of these qualities).

These qualities will be addressed in the coming chapters.

Yoga begins with humility.

We can see how genuinely non-violent Arjuna and his family were throughout their lives: for decades they tolerated so much from their envious, evil cousins, the Kurus – now the opposing army on the battlefield of Kuruksetra. The Pandavas always wanted to take the higher road, and preferred humility and the shelter of each others' divine natures – and that of their friend Krishna's – to the alternative of fighting for what was rightfully theirs, fighting even for the benefit of others, and further, fighting to uphold truth and integrity.

They gave opportunities time and again to their enemies to change, to make things right, to act according to higher principles, but all in vain. And ultimately they did fight. As Krishna told Arjuna, sometimes you have to stand and fight.

Genuine peace isn't possible unless there is the development of real knowledge, divine qualities and spiritual principles that both Krishna and Patanjali speak of. As already mentioned, Krishna refers to peace in the second chapter: 'One who is not connected with the Supreme can have neither transcendental intelligence nor a steady mind, without which there is no possibility of peace. And how can there be any happiness without peace?'

When we speak of non-violence, we must do so from the platform of knowledge, we must ensure we can identify it and understand the difference between genuine ahimsa and ignorance.

CHAPTER 4

Satya

Truth

Everything, and everyone, depends on truth…

SATYA IS MORE THAN JUST a matter of speaking the truth. It is also more than a desirable habit or even a lifestyle to adopt.

Where truth is concerned, there isn't even a single truth. Everyone has their own truth. We often hear people say, 'Well, that is *your* truth, how *you* see things, and I accept that, but someone else's truth might be different.' Sounds reasonable enough, because everyone has a different angle of vision.

But is there such a thing as just plain 'truth'?

We can answer this question by first establishing the principles of this yama. While details can be adjusted and altered, flex themselves to adapt to an individual or situation, principles are not open to alteration or adjustment, and nor are they changeable according to the conditioned perspective of an individual. Satya is one such principle. While it may adjust its parameters to incorporate the details of time, place or circumstance, its essence, or the principle of truth, always remains the same. Now, what is this essence? Satya is a quality inherent in one's spiritual nature. While Patanjali first mentions satya in his *Yoga Sutras* as the second yama, he elaborates on it a few verses later when he talks about *satyam-pratisthayam*, being situated in truth. Patanjali explains that the yoga practitioner does not simply adopt truthful principles when or if it suits, or use it in a superficial manner. Satya has to do with one's behaviour and consciousness; it is an inner path that is lit always by the principle of truth, in action, word and mind. Dedicated yoga practitioners know, and practise, the essence of the principle.

Yoga means knowing and understanding saram, or essence.

In the same way, Krishna speaks of truth to Arjuna in the Gita while citing the qualities that indicate an enlightened person. (I have mentioned these in the previous yama, ahimsa.) Bhaktivedanta Swami, in his elaborate commentaries on these verses, speaks of satya in a practical sense: 'This word means that one should not distort the truth for some personal interest...one should hear from an authority. One should not construe some interpretation for his personal interest.'

In other words, we accept the essence of truth, and do not add our own personal slant to it. Being 'situated in truth' means not speculating on what truth is or giving our own interpretation or opinion, but understanding that it is directed by a principle. This principle is that it must come from a divine source. This is the *basic* principle of truth. From this principle stem others, which direct our thought, speech and actions.

As we learnt in the first section of this book, as yoga practitioners we are immediately in a position where we are seeking direction from an authority: we learn the theories, principles and practices of yoga. Yet, we see around us constantly the result of people twisting an ancient philosophy and system to suit their own ends, quite a contrary behaviour to what Patanjali and Krishna both speak of. This is unfortunate, yet understandable, for we are flawed human beings with propensities that override those innate, divine instincts that we desire so much to nurture and develop.

So how do we avoid the pitfalls of distorting the truth for our personal interests?

In chapter 10 of the Gita, Krishna tells Arjuna that 'intelligence, knowledge, freedom from doubt and delusion, forgiveness, truthfulness, control of the senses, control of the mind' and other qualities (which we will focus on later) are the qualities of a good human being. In that vein, Patanjali specifies truth as one of the 'ethical guidelines' in one's yoga practice. Bhaktivedanta Swami elaborates succinctly in his commentary on Krishna's words: 'According to social conventions, it is said that one can speak the truth only when it is palatable to others. But that is not truthfulness. The truth should be spoken in a straightforward way, so that others will understand actually what the facts are... Although sometimes the truth is unpalatable, one should not refrain from speaking it. Truthfulness demands that the facts be presented as they are for the benefit of others.'

In order to live a life of truth, we have to ensure that the principle of truth is flowing through our thoughts, words and actions. As we have understood, the source of truth is the Divine. As Patanjali phrases it, one has to be 'situated in truth,' and as Bhaktivedanta Swami explains it, truth must be spoken for the benefit of others, regardless of how 'unpalatable' it may appear. Truth, therefore, is not flexible.

Truth is knowledge that is divine in nature. It is the knowledge of how to behave, knowledge that teaches us how to counter the negative emotions and thoughts that assail us, and the knowledge that gives us freedom from the miseries that life inflicts upon us. Truth is what Krishna is speaking to Arjuna in the Gita, and it is embodied by action, thought and deed that serve knowledge, are replete with knowledge, that enlighten and soothe, that guide and direct. This is satya. We may find different avenues to explore, understand and live truth, but that doesn't change its essence.

This might sound right in theory, but how is this to be lived? There are not many who are willing to speak or hear the truth. For instance, while the majority of people might claim to want the truth, most, when they hear it, do not appreciate what they are hearing if it is unpalatable to them in some way. Those in a position to speak tend to give more consideration to protecting the sensibilities of the hearer, or regard their own reputation as being more important than telling the truth. Bending the truth to promote one's own interests is a common human weakness.

Knowing how to find the truth and how to recognize it is crucial. Krishna spoke to Arjuna of this, and it was covered in the first section of this book. In particular, Krishna spoke of the principle of truth – what it really is and what it stems from, grows into, looks, sounds and feels like – and that truth has to be firmly established in our inner worlds and psyches, and then in the outer world.

We can define this yama of satya by summarizing what we have read and learnt from Krishna's teachings to Arjuna so far: it is a principle that directs our thoughts, speech and actions; its essence is divine knowledge, not mental speculation or opinion; and it benefits us and others when it is thought, spoken or acted. It may not be easy or palatable, but it is beneficial.

Thus, when we are situated in truth, as Patanjali writes, and when we are operating from the platform of truth, as Krishna explains, then we have no fear in speaking or living the truth. Our truth can more accurately be described as 'opinion'. Satya, on the other hand, is that graceful principle whose deep roots blossom and guide us to live truthfully, think truthfully, and reflect in our behaviour those inner qualities being developed, relied upon and integrated into everything we come in contact with. That is satya.

CHAPTER 5

Asteya
Integrity

Looking 'within' for one's contentment,
not 'without'...

I WAS LOOKING FORWARD to writing about this yama, researching and reading the many and varied ways the word 'asteya', integrity, is translated or understood, both in Eastern and Western philosophy. I discovered that Westerners are content to relate this yama to the Christian commandment of 'thou shalt not steal', as asteya is often referred to in Western translations as 'non-stealing'.

However, this meaning is rather limited as asteya is, in fact, a good deal more than that. In the ancient Sanskrit text, *Manu Samhita*, we find asteya included in what are described as the ten characteristics of religiosity, a source of higher moral codes similar to Patanjali's yamas and niyamas.

Although this book is not the place for a dissection and discussion of these ten characteristics, it is nonetheless interesting to note that as recently as the eighteenth century, a noted Vedic author, Bhaktivinoda Thakura, wrote that while six of those characteristics were 'directed towards oneself', the remaining four were 'obligations towards others': kshama, forgiveness; asteya, integrity; satya, truthfulness; and akrodha, freedom from anger.[1] It is also wonderful to see in the same text that 'satya' and 'asteya', truth and integrity, are two separate qualities, whereas in the syntax of the English language, they are often used as different words for the same quality. Clearly, in a deeper sense, they are not the same.

---

[1] The other six characteristics are explained in the portion of Bhaktivinoda Thakura's *Jaiva Dharma*, which is about the ten characteristics of religion as listed in *Manu-samhita*: "'The ten characteristics of religiosity are *dhrtih*, contentment; *ksama*, forgiveness, that is not revenging a wrong; *dama*, self-control, that is remaining in control of the mind in spite of the presence of allurements; *asteya*, honesty; *saucam*, cleanliness; *indriya-nigraha*, withdrawing the senses from sense objects; *dhih*, scriptural knowledge; *vidya*, education, that is knowledge of the soul; *satyam*, truthfulness, that is awareness of reality; and *akrodha*, freedom from anger, that is to be not angered when provoked.

"Of these, *dhrtih*, contentment; *dama*, self-control; *sauca*, cleanliness; *indriya-nigraha*, withdrawing the senses; *dhih*, scriptural knowledge; and *vidya*, knowledge of the soul are the six duties and characteristics directed towards oneself. Whereas, *ksama*, forgiveness; *asteya*, honesty; *satyam*, truthfulness; and *akrodha*, freedom from anger, are the four obligations towards others. However, the duty of worshipping the Supreme Lord, Sri Hari, is not clearly delineated in any of these ten characteristics, which have been enumerated to encourage us in following the moral religious principles. Furthermore, it cannot be said that human life becomes pure and perfect by only developing these characteristics.'" *Jaiva Dharma* was written in 1893 and translated by Bhaktivedanta Library Services.

Yoga embodies the holistic concept of integrity.

Yoga is about being honest and virtuous, upstanding, true to one's self and those around us. In other words, it is a rather hard quality to confine to one word, at least in English.

Most readers are somewhat familiar with the Upanishads, or at least know that they stem from the vast library of Vedic literature. In what is perhaps my favourite, the Sri Isopanisad, the first verse succinctly describes this principle of asteya as 'living virtuously and not taking more than our due'. We are talking about a lack of greed, satisfaction with what one has, honesty, integrity…you get the picture.

I like how the understanding of asteya unfolds in the Gita. Arjuna is in a turmoil the likes of which we are never likely to experience. He has more than a right to fight: he has a duty. Yet he says in the first chapter when he is expressing his doubts to Krishna, 'Sin will overcome us if we slay such aggressors. What would we gain, and how could we be happy by killing our own kinsmen?' Arjuna is actually contemplating living by begging rather than fighting unnecessarily. He even says to Krishna, 'It is better to die than to live wonderfully by the results of killing.'

Therefore, these two choices were what Arjuna felt he was limited to in an effort to resolve the dilemma he faced. He was in all respects, a virtuous man, a man of integrity, a man situated firmly in asteya. His desire to live the life of a beggar, although he was a prince and warrior, is evidence of the control he exercised over his senses, ego and mind, and a sign of his highly-developed quality of detachment.

Yoga means instilling our duties with the principle of integrity.

Yet, these choices, according to Krishna, stemmed from what he called Arjuna's 'ignorance'. Surely to a man of principle, a man who lived his life according to the path of dharma, the option he was contemplating was based on integrity? On dharma itself?

Arjuna had already acted according to his dharma and acted with integrity when he committed to both his wife, Draupadi, and to Krishna to punish the Kauravas for their crimes before the battle of Kurukshetra began.

Before the Kurukshetra war, the Kurus had, over a period of many years, tricked their royal cousins out of their reign; they had disrobed Draupadi in a public court; they had driven Arjuna and his brothers out of their kingdom, banished them to the forest, and burned down the home in which they had taken shelter; they had pillaged the treasury of the former royal family; they had tried to poison Bhima, Arjuna's brother, and had attacked Arjuna and his brothers with deadly weapons on several occasions – the final insult being now, on the battlefield of Kurukshetra, where the battalions of the Kuru dynasty stood before Arjuna, ready for war.

In the Vedic culture and according to the scriptures that Arjuna and his brother – the ruler of Bharata, Maharaja Yudhisthira – lived by, it is said that there are six actions that permit one to take the life of an aggressor: when they attack with deadly weapons, when they occupy your land, when they try to poison you, when they steal your property, when they abduct your wife, and when they set fire to your property. The Kuru cousins had committed all six offences against the Pandava family. Arjuna, firmly and resolutely fixed in his dharma, had vowed to avenge them as was his duty.

Thus, his moment of weakness on the battlefield, when he turned to Krishna and said, 'I will not fight' was, as Krishna explained during the course of their lengthy conversation, based on fear, confusion, and grief: it was a decision made in ignorance. Krishna explains clearly throughout the ensuing dialogue that when one is fixed in knowledge and when the intelligence is steady, then one can act in truth, and with integrity. But when one is controlled by the mind and senses, one cannot know right from wrong.

So while Arjuna's choice to give up fighting may have seemed like a decision based on dharma and decided upon in the mood of integrity, it was not so. He had already acted in these ways when he committed to the battle, and that previous decision was the right one. Thus, his admitted weakness was just that: a moment of human frailty.

So how do we deal with our own frailties when doubts and obstacles assail us? How do we learn what level of integrity we possess, how it functions, how it develops and how it works in our daily lives?

Krishna specifically and repeatedly refers to a quality that allows us to acknowledge, carry and deal with our human flaws. This is a key ingredient in acquiring the ability to act with integrity, in thought, word and deed. This quality is humility. Patanjali also stresses on this in the *Yoga Sutras.*

Yoga begins with humility.

Arjuna shows us what humility is. Despite his intelligence being overwhelmed, and being consumed with grief and confusion, he still had the humility to turn to someone he knew would guide him properly, ensure that his decisions were based in truth and integrity, and support him to the very end, no matter what the outcome.

I saw on an American yoga website how one profile-happy, fame-seeking yoga teacher was promoting herself as a yogi. Stating 'I'm a yogi', all the while slandering famous people and their yoga practices, arrogantly proclaiming herself superior to others and deriding anyone who questioned her, did not make for a 'yogi' as far as I was concerned. Integrity? No. Humility? Zero. Yogi? Never!

As seen through Arjuna, these qualities of humility, truth and integrity intertwine and weave themselves through the consciousness, mind, speech and actions. This is why Patanjali knew that the principles he outlined in the yamas and niyamas formed the foundation of yoga.

Mantra chanting, meditation and other spiritual methods prepare the mind and heart for the practice of yogasana. Integrity, however, does not grow from physical exercise. It develops in the cultivated heart and mind of one who practices the personal, devotional elements of yoga along with their asanas.

Ultimately, Arjuna's decision to fight was far, far beyond what he had initially understood to be the proper moral path – refusing to kill the army that had assembled before him. But obviously there is more to life than following moral roadmaps. Knowing the divine source, the essence of all creation, is what Krishna says is real knowledge.

Patanjali's yamas and niyamas are mere starting blocks. They do not make us or our yoga practice 'spiritual', and nor do they make us yogis. They are just the beginning of a way of life, the foundation, as it were.

CHAPTER 6

Brahmacharya

Abstience

The harmony created by purity of thought,
word and deed

THE SUN HAS NOT *yet risen. I sit on the wide verandah and watch as the village comes to life the same way it does every day, and has done for thousands of years. Pilgrims and locals alike, chanting, singing and reciting prayers, walk along the dusty road that circles the sacred town of Vrindavan. It is only 4 a.m. but the road has seen a constant stream of pedestrian traffic for hours, possibly all night.*

They are an ocean of colour on the track: bright and beautiful swathes of cloth on a group of Rajasthani ladies; yogis in saffron, their dreadlocked hair piled high on their heads; a trio of Brijbasi ladies in varying shades of blue-green. Like a wave of liquid love they all come, their mouths uttering the names of Radha and Krishna, intent on their mission of encircling the village in the cool hours of the early morning.

The three young children appear from nowhere. The oldest, a girl of around 11 years, leads her siblings: a brother who looks to be about 8 years old and a sister of about 6. They follow in the footsteps of the yogis, locals, pilgrims and dedicated spiritualists, carrying thin padded mats that they place on the ground, to prostrate fully – the sacred act of 'dandavat parikrama'. Then they rise up again and walk a few steps, only to repeat their act of prayer all over again. This way, they go around the sacred village, offering their respects to the town, its residents, temples, deities, trees, rivers, kundas. This is a mammoth task for an adult, and literally other-worldly for a child.

The children are unaccompanied. No parent is forcing them; they are not part of a group. Three in a row, they carry their little mats and bow down repeatedly, making a few small feet of progress over the minutes that I watch them. Their faces are peaceful and they are silent; their clothes are old and dusty, the only kind to wear for such an endeavour.

Slowly, they make their way along the track, becoming dots in the distance and then moving out of sight completely.

For many, the word 'abstinence' conjures up an image of suffering; a dry, unfulfilled life of repression, denial, fear and longing. For most, the battle of the senses is a lifelong one, fought on the inner fields of the mind, escaping through the rocky trails of longing and desire, not only in a sexual sense but materially too, hankering for more, wanting to increase and expand the possibility of enjoyment in the fields of play.

The sight of three young children voluntarily, even joyfully, executing what most adults would consider the most arduous task they could undertake, was breathtaking. I watched in awe as these children tracked their way around the sacred town in an ageless expression of love and devotion.

These children, I knew, were three brahmacharya adults in the making. The control of their child-senses was supreme, and their content and peaceful demeanour belied the suggestion that they were doing something they didn't want to do, as children often feel. I could write thousands of words on the principles of abstinence were I so inclined, but these three children surpass any written word.

In the Gita, Krishna says of brahmacharya, 'Austerity of the body consists in worshipping the Supreme Lord, the brahmanas, the spiritual master and superiors like the father and mother, and in cleanliness, simplicity, celibacy and non-violence' (17:14).

These three little yogis had perfected austerity of the body, but austerity of the body requires the austerity of the mind. The children weren't distracted or bored or unwilling: their minds had already attained an obvious state of acceptance of the physical austerity they were performing. Their 'abstinence in action' was worthy of an advanced yogi's behavior.

While Patanjali's *Yoga Sutras* refer to brahmacharya as 'sexual non-expressiveness', its essence is based not only on abstaining from sex but on controlling the mind and the senses. Abstinence is far more than a physical state; it stems from the mental, emotional and psychological planes in a person.

When we speak of this yama of abstinence, it is important to remember the time in which Patanjali wrote the *Yoga Sutras* was centuries ago, when the four varnas or orders of life were practised as a standard: brahmacharya, adolesence or student life; grhastha, householder life; varnaprastha, withdrawal from material life, or retirement; and sannyasa, renunciation from life.

Today, these varnas are a little harder to detect in society; less people are following these social orders. It is important to note, too, that in such a social order, brahmacharys were young, in the prime of youth; they were under the tutelage of a teacher or guru, they were educated in cultural and philosophical matters, they studied scripture, and gradually developed into fine young men, some of whom would marry and have families, some who would remain celibate their whole lives and eventually take to sannyasa.

So is this yama even relevant in today's world? It certainly is, and that is where the solid roots of this yama – the mental, emotional and psychological roots that make the physical act of abstinence possible – come into play.

Yoga means a foundation of strength built with spiritual principles.

When we read of, learn about and try to live these yamas and niyamas, we should remember that we are not taking them up for the sake of it; nor are we taking up one and not the others. When we read about abstinence, we are not reading of it as a stand-alone subject but as a small part of a larger philosophy or teaching. In other words, it is but a portion of the solid base that becomes our foundation in yoga. This foundation is made up of the principles of all the yamas and niyamas: truth, cleanliness, non-violence, integrity, and so on. Brahmacharya is a principle, and in these modern times, it can be practised by men, women, married people or those who are single, and even children.

We are all familiar with the powerful demands of the mind and senses. We can be convinced to do anything, indulge in anything, anytime, anywhere, by our mind and senses. Abstinence means to curb one's indulgences. While for a few it may indeed mean a life of celibacy, for the majority it does not. It simply asks of us that we are conscious of our thoughts, words and actions, and that we become aware of our behaviour and our myriad desires, learning to control what can create obstacles or distract us from our yoga practice, both externally and internally.

Brahmacharya means, in essence, to be simple in behaviour. Indeed, there is much said in the Gita about self-control. While brahmacharya is one word, it is without doubt defined by, and embodies, a whole world of smaller and larger acts, thoughts and principles, as I have explained above.

CHAPTER 7

Aparigraha

Non-possessiveness

Refining and balancing our basic needs

'NON-POSSESSIVENESS' IS PERHAPS MY favourite translation of aparigraha, as it embodies a broader understanding: whatever comes our way, either in a gross or subtle form, is not our property but simply what is due to us in this lifetime. It is not ours to pursue, long for or possess. In terms of explaining 'what is due to us,' we can refer to the verse from Sri Isopanisad quoted in the last section, that 'one should therefore accept only those things necessary for himself, which are set aside as his quota.'

To accumulate more than is reasonably necessary for us to live on and to be motivated by greed is contrary to the yama of aparigraha. This is not simply some 'nice' way to behave; it actually develops one's character, and enhances the quality of aparigraha.

Yoga purifies one's mind, senses, and activities.

In truth, the only thing we possess is our individual identity, which means that in this life, our priority is the purification of material existence so we are able to enter into our spiritual one.

Again, we come back to control of the mind and senses. In chapter 14, Krishna says that 'from the mode of passion, greed develops'. The energy that leaves the body in the form of the subtle mind and goes seeking external fulfilment or expression must finally be contained; it should be turned back into our own self-examination. We cannot stop or renounce this energy's existence: we can, however, direct it for our own benefit, that is, our spiritual benefit, not our material gain.

Eventually, we arrive at the real meaning of this quality of aparigraha: self-containment. Krishna says that it is impossible to understand him unless we understand his energies, and by energies he means both material and spiritual. So, in the same way, we cannot hope to understand ourselves or our motives for doing something unless we understand our own energy.

Yoga means elevating the consciousness.

In his commentary on the above-mentioned verse, Bhaktivedanta Swami says '...if the world is devoted to the modes of passion and ignorance, there can be no peace or prosperity.' He explains: 'One can see that even if one has enough money and adequate arrangements for sense gratification, there is neither happiness nor peace of mind.'

In fact, Bhaktivedanta Swami was a good example of aparigraha. At one stage in his life, he was one of the wealthiest men in the world, with properties and land all over the globe, publishing houses worldwide, and tens of thousands of people selling the books he translated and published. Yet, not a single penny was in his name in any personal bank account. He lived simply. Despite travelling the world, he carried just a small bag with a few articles of clothing. At home in India, he usually lived in a mud hut with a grass roof when he had the most opulent and luxurious facilities at his disposal.

This brings us to the most crucial point in Krishna's teachings on greed when, in chapter 16, he tells Arjuna, 'There are three gates leading to hell: lust, anger and greed. Every sane man should give these up, for they lead to the degradation of the soul.'

The degradation of the soul. While no amount of yogasanas will 'save one's soul', the living and practising of yoga can, combining both the physical aspect (through asanas) and the spiritual aspect (through bhakti), elevating the consciousness through the material elements of ignorance and passion to the mode of goodness and, from there, to transcendence.

But...

I got to this point and read what I had written. Anyone can 'write' about yoga, its practices and its goals, as well as talk about yamas and niyamas. But who can actually live them?

Yoga means simple living and high thinking.

The truth is that while all this sounds simple and concise, such simplicity is *really* hard. Simple living and high thinking inhabit a level of existence that very few people in the world can lay claim to. And those who aspire to it find it even more difficult to achieve due to the state of the world, the frenetic pace of life, the technological ease available to us, and all those other things in life that daily present themselves as obstacles to self-containment.

But it is a worthy endeavour. It is what our yoga practice is leading towards, and so there is nothing to do *but* endeavour. To conclude, Krishna says to Arjuna, 'In this endeavour there is no loss or diminution. A little advancement on this path can protect one from the most dangerous type of fear.'

CHAPTER 8

Saucham
Purity

Sowing the seeds of a pure mind and practice

AS WE MEANDER THROUGH the yamas and watch their deeper meaning unfold in the course of the Gita's discussions on them, we start to see a pattern. The yamas are intertwined, all dependent on and supportive of each other.

This first niyama, purity, showcases this and is a clear example of a foundational understanding:

Yoga creates the foundation for, and is dependent upon, the practice of purity.

So what does purity actually mean? As we have seen several times through the course of Krishna's talks with Arjuna, and through scrutinizing each quality of Patanjali's yamas and niyamas, Sanskrit words tend to have more than just their basic definition and a direct translation; they embody a set of principles. The Oxford English Dictionary gives two definitions of 'purity': 'freedom from contamination' and 'freedom from immorality'. 'Freedom from immorality' is in line with the more subtle definition of both the Gita and the *Yoga Sutras*, meaning that the mind, consciousness and senses are all in an uncontaminated state; they are clean and unobstructed.

In modern times, this is a challenge for everyone. Television, magazines, movies and the digital world serve to actually sully our thoughts and our consciousness, bombarding us with graphic images about every kind of material object and desire we can possibly dream of, letting us know in no uncertain terms that if we do not satisfy those (endless) desires, we shall be deeply unhappy people.

In chapter 17 of the Gita, Krishna mentions most of the yamas and niyamas, including our first niyama, purity. He tells Arjuna that peacefulness, self-control, austerity, purity, tolerance, honesty, wisdom, knowledge and religiousness are the qualities a yoga practitioner – a spiritual practitioner – seeks to develop.

We have looked at some of these concepts in the yamas already covered: self-control and austerity, honesty and integrity, and peacefulness. As we read them, we are encouraged to develop them. Those qualities that already sit within us are given the opportunity to rise to the surface; we are enthused to nurture them and cultivate more of the same quality, or its neighbouring, complementary qualities.

In this way, they weave through each other and together

produce a beautiful and rich tapestry that becomes the artful expression of our spiritual desires and qualities. They become the face we show the world, they become second nature, and Bhaktivedanta Swami says, 'we seek to make something our second nature, then by practise it becomes our first nature.' This is what we actually wish to achieve when we read of these qualities and principles – that they become our 'first nature'.

Krishna then says, '...serenity, simplicity, gravity, self-control and purity of thought are the austerities of the mind.' While the world speaks of five senses – sight, hearing, touch, taste and smell – the Gita explains that actually there are six senses, and the most powerful is the mind. So in this way we understand that on one level, the physical level, 'purity' means cleanliness; and on an internal level, it means the cleanliness of the mind, controlling the inputs to the mind so that it is free from the contamination of day-to-day life. More will be discussed in the section on the third niyama, austerity, but as mentioned above, these qualities and principles are interdependent, the one before serves the one ahead, and vice versa; they support and enhance each other. So it is that purity goes hand in hand with a little austerity.

Yoga means controlling the senses by willingly,
carefully and joyfully soliciting the inputs to the mind
and maintaining purity of content.

Again, it is that difficult task of keeping it simple. Everywhere we look, there are always willing assailants of the mind and the senses. How do we keep them at bay?

As the yamas and niyamas are intertwined, so are all the other concepts and elements of Vedic or Vaishnava philosophy. Here, I would like to bring in the concept of karma. While we won't delve into a philosophical treatise on the subject, we do need to acknowledge that attaining a level of purity – of consciousness, mind, thought, speech, action and reaction – requires an understanding of karma, and how every action we take has a negative or positive reaction.

In terms of purity of thought, mind and consciousness, what goes into our thoughts and consciousness is what comes out in our thoughts, speech, and action. The famous scientist Isaac Newton, with his third law of gravity, was possibly as close to explaining karma – even unknowingly – as anyone has come: that 'for every action, there is an equal and opposite reaction.' What we put out there comes back to us in an equal or opposite way. If we do good things, good comes to us; if we do bad things, bad comes to us. This is a simplistic and incomplete definition of karma, but it gives the basic understanding that to balance our thoughts, words and actions, some 'filtering' is required, a conscious endeavour to keep the self 'clean.'

In terms of the niyama of purity, we are speaking of karmic reactions upon the mind and senses, which infect the consciousness, direct thoughts, determine actions and result in either good or bad consequences for these aspects of the self.

Yoga means consciousnessly cultivating purity, which does not appear of its own accord.

As already mentioned, purity means both physical cleanliness and an internal cleanliness of the self. Without its physical manifestation, there is no chance of purity establishing itself as part of the character. In other words, again, what goes in is what comes out. Yoga is not possible while a person is eating meat or other by-products of violence. Yes, you can do the asanas, but you are not practicing yoga. Without living the finer, more subtle elements of the yamas and niyamas – the qualities that Patanjali says form the character of the yoga practitioner – one is merely performing exercises.

Yoga is a science, a manner of being, a conscious and pure form of life-practice.

Yoga incorporates physical aspects: asana, breath work, bodily health and cleanliness; and it incorporates the subtler elements of the human body: mind, consciousness, habits – both good and bad, along with a higher level of thought, speech and behaviour. Consequently, a disregard for even one of the elements of yoga, while a voluntary or personal choice, is not an intelligent one.

The process and perfection of yoga does not bend, flex and adjust its parameters to accommodate those who prefer to water it down or minimize its purity and force. If the practitioner is still swayed by the lower modes of ignorance and passion and not by goodness, they consequently will not enter into the practice of yoga or gain the full benefits such a process offers. This is how we understand that even a 'small thing' like one niyama or one yama is actually something that contributes to the whole and is, in and of itself, important.

CHAPTER 9

Santosh

Contentment

What we see externally is not always an indication of what lies beneath…

TO BE HONEST, I do not know many content people. I know some who want to be content but don't know how to accomplish this; I know others who are trying to be, but find it difficult; and we all know some who pretend to be content, but who really aren't – we find that there is always something lacking or lurking beneath the surface.

Yet at the same time there are some who might appear to be discontented but who, deep down, actually are at peace. Some are not able to recognize the difference, so they criticize them and say that they are disturbed or unsettled. Those critics do not perceive the inner depths of contentment which, while lurking underneath the myriad issues and problems the world dumps on us on a daily basis, are very real and which sustain one in an otherwise disturbed world.

If that sounds confusing, let's look at it this way: the world is difficult – that much we can all agree on. Sometimes, we may look at others and make superficial judgements about them. To us, some people may appear to be disturbed. But, if we look a little closer, we find we are wrong, that while the world and daily life may disturb those people at a surface level, deep down they understand that it doesn't change who they really are, that their 'inner peace' is very real and sustains them. In short, 'don't judge a book by its cover.' Success, achievement and consistency do actually take a certain amount of energy and passion. And passion has its own character, its own qualities.

Yoga means one's intelligence is guided by the yoga process; it does not dwell in the temporary realm of the senses.

That we are discussing yogic qualities and aspiring to acquire them does not mean that we become little 'saints', or that we change our personality or adopt some false persona to impress others. It means *adding* the yogic qualities to our lives, becoming more conscious of them, nurturing and honing them so they become our habits.

Nothing satisfies a person who is filled with discontent; they complain about everything, and even when something good happens, you will hear them saying, 'Well, it might be nice, but it won't last...' or other such negative responses. Yet, we all go through periods of deep discontentment sometimes, when nothing satisfies us, when we feel that we're not getting anywhere in our lives.

How do we end this cycle of negativity and achieve actual contentment? Is it even possible? The answer is yes, of course it is possible. Let's look again at one point that has been presented several times in this book:

> *Yoga ultimately means devotion, without which one's yoga practice remains bound to the physical realm, where there is no chance of peace.*

Oftentimes, those who are self-absorbed or only interested in their own happiness or success are not actually content people. Moreover, they are not even really very nice. They try to appear to be so, because this world is ruled by political correctness and falsity. But they are not truly peaceful or satisfied. What satisfies the soul is not what satisfies the senses, especially those ruled by a self-interested mind.

As I previously mentioned, the yamas and niyamas support and are simultaneously dependent on each other. Without purity, for example, none of the other yamas and niyamas are possible. By contrast, santosh is not possible without the niyamas that lie *ahead* of it, specifically, studying sacred texts and being God-conscious.

Certainly one might argue that contentment is available in so many forms. Perhaps deep contentment is found in your yoga practice. Or in being with your child or family. Or going for long walks. But without these two transcendental elements – real knowledge from sacred texts and God-consciousness, contentment will not be a permanent state within, a part of one's being.

Yoga is a process that transfoms the human being at every level.

An animal is different from a human being, for contentment is confined to the range of perception and intelligence that comes with a body and consequently, its inner contentment is confined to the senses being sated. How many times have you heard someone say, 'I want to come back as a dog'? Or an eagle, or a dolphin?

But is that really contentment? More like escapism, cleverly disguised ignorance, or a desire for just plain peace and quiet. Which is all quite understandable. But the material aspects of an individual need to be elevated from their customary business of satisfying the demands of the body and mind to altering the very consciousness. This is the only way one can arrive at the source of real contentment possible for the human being.

There is no mention of the word santosh in the Gita, but the root word of santosh is one that yoga students are even more familiar with: shanti. Bhaktivedanta Swami says, 'Real peace can be obtained only in that transcendental stage of existence. That is the state of real contentment.' During a talk he gave in Los Angeles in 1976, he elaborated further on this point: 'What is contentment? If you have unsolved problems, that is an ass's contentment. An ass does not know how to check death. He does not think of it. But a human being's intelligence says whether the disease can be checked, whether the death can be checked. That is a human being. The ass cannot think. If we remain contented like an ass, so that is animal life.'

Finally, our purpose in practicing yoga – both the external and internal elements of the practice – is to become better human beings. As has been mentioned, the Gita is like the handbook for the human life, and Patanjali's *Yoga Sutras* certainly fall into the same category. Even studying both books and understanding how to practically apply them means we are already on the path to the highest realm of human existence that we can reach. Learning to apply the teachings to each moment of our lives – that is the process of yoga.

CHAPTER 10

Tapas

Austerity

THIS NIYAMA IS ABOUT austerity. In the lives we lead, we don't really see much in the way of learning how to be austere. Yes, many of us deal with financial hardships, and the term 'austerity' is usually aligned with financial restriction. But tapas is a much larger concept.

Krishna elaborates beautifully on austerity in chapter 17 of the Gita, and it is one of my favourite sections because it addresses the consciousness or motive behind a person's actions.

But what *is* 'austerity'? It's not simply a dreadlocked yogi in the Himalayas sitting on a bed of nails, or the other typical images that come to mind sometimes when we hear the word spoken. Austerity can perhaps be most easily described these days as a 'determined undertaking'. When we set out to achieve something, we immediately understand that there are things we must give up or sacrifice, or things we must take on, be able to do, all of which are quite apart from our normal daily routines. Professional or Olympic athletes, for example, undergo great feats of austerity to achieve their goals: training, more training, even more training, dietary restrictions and little or no social life. There are many varied forms of 'determined undertaking' we may engage in during the course of our lives which, as part of their nature or character, are 'austerity'.

But Krishna reminds us of the three primary characteristics that determine what the result of our austerity will be: ignorance, passion, and goodness. As you know, our minds and senses are also affected by these three modes of material energy, and our actions and their consequences, are categorized in the same way. Of course, we want to avoid the first two modes of ignorance and passion.

We sometimes hear that it is not possible to understand a person's motives, or that it is judgemental to consider what another's motives are. That may be true, yet in terms of observing another's yoga practice, it becomes clear what Krishna is speaking of in regard to austerity in ignorance or in passion, and he explains the symptoms to Arjuna:

- Austerities performed foolishly by means of obstinate self-torture or to destroy or injure others are said to be in the mode of ignorance.
- Ostentatious austerities performed in order to gain respect, honour and reverence are said to be in the mode of passion, and are neither stable nor permanent.
- The austerities of body, mind and speech, done not for

one's own pleasure but for the benefit of the Supreme, are considered to be in the mode of goodness.

Ignorance is easy to identify. In yoga, it most often means that one is pushing oneself beyond one's physical capabilities, causing injury (or the possibility of injury) by considering that what one is doing is for a good outcome, despite the warning signs the body might be sending. It clearly is not for a 'good outcome.'

Passion is similarly easy to identify: yoga, or other forms of health and exercise, often see people who adopt a 'show pony' approach, pushing themselves forward as the prime example of how to achieve something, how to look or act. Again, this is not the goal.

Goodness stems from what we have covered extensively in this book: the internal aspects of yoga – the development of qualities that hone our character – are what contribute to a holistic yoga practice. *This* is the goal we are seeking.

Sometimes I speak with people who, as lifelong renunciates and/or celibates in different spiritual systems, express the fear that their austerities will trip them up in their later years, that as life passes they will begin to long for the love and romance they so readily and energetically renounced in their youth.

Then there are people who came to their spiritual path later, taking up a life of celibacy and renunciation after a tumultuous, passionate youth. Their fear is that the memories of love and romance will come back to haunt them in their later years, tormenting them with feelings of impurity and inadequacy, or even as temptations all over again.

But when we are practising yoga, when we are developing the qualities Patanjali and Krishna both speak of, there is – as Krishna taught Arjuna right in the beginning – no need to fear. Or, more specifically, there is no need to fear the result or outcome of what we do when our intelligence is balanced and we make decisions in a grounded and informed way.

Yoga subjugates fear.

As Krishna tells Arjuna in chapter 4, fear is a symptom of ignorance. The fear of being haunted by one's youth or a longing for what we might have missed in our youth, are both performed in the mode of passion or ignorance, and consequently result again in passion or ignorance. Therefore, to long for what we think we missed out on stems from a state of passion, and to fear we will be haunted by the past stems from ignorance.

But where is our ability to live balanced wisdom in our youth? It is a rare thing to experience or witness an event like that of the three children who I saw performing their austerities in Vrindavan. Apart from these rare examples, do we assume wisdom to be a sign of 'age'? Perhaps. It can be said, however, that the decision to follow any yoga practice, be it bhakti, jnana or ashtanga, is evidence of wisdom and an austerity performed in the mode of goodness. There is, however, a caveat here.

The initial desire to take up yoga could be based on fear, for example, the fear of being judged by our peers for being lazy, or the fear of falling ill. But yoga itself is situated in the mode of goodness. That's quite a statement, so how do we justify it? Because, as with everything else, a practice or a method or an event is judged by its qualities – the same way we can assess ourselves and what mode of material nature we are influenced by. I think by now, at this point of our progress through the Gita and the *Yoga Sutras,* it is fair to say we can easily assess what mode we are influenced by in anything we do throughout the day. Even if we are motivated by fear to take up yoga, the result will be there as long as we are aware of the subtleties of our actions and why we do things.

For example, Krishna tells Arjuna his decision not to fight is evidence that he is influenced by the mode of ignorance. And, as mentioned, whatever action or method we undertake has its own qualities too: the pastime of watching horror movies for hours on end while drinking alcohol is in the mode of ignorance. That might be an extreme example but deliberately given so that we can understand that this action, its qualities and its results are in the mode of ignorance.

In the same way, we can understand that yoga – not our *practice* of it but yoga itself – is a methodology that embodies the mode of goodness. When we practice yoga, we enter into an environment that is encouraging *us* to also be in the mode of goodness, an environment that embodies goodness. Certainly we can redirect that – as with the example of 'hot' modern yoga – to something lesser, to something in the mode of passion. But when we step up to our yoga practice in its true form, we should be consciously aware that we have before us the opportunity to engage in an activity in the mode of goodness.

Yoga is the practice of controlling the mind and senses.

And, in the end, this is the crux of the issue, our greatest austerity in life: controlling the mind and senses. It is a lifelong practice in youth, in married life, in school, at work, socially, with family, and we have to live it no matter who we are, where we live, how rich or poor, how young or old we are. We can live simply, live a life with minimal complications, but still this austerity exists. We might be billionaires but that situation, too, requires control of the mind and senses – austerity all over again. Perhaps the austerity in this billionaire lifestyle is not the same 'flavour' as the less fortunate experience, but austerity is present in everything.

There is so much that can disturb us if we let it. We may speak of doing things in the mode of goodness, which elevates the consciousness, mind, senses; a practice that contributes to the development of all the qualities and principles we are studying in this handbook. In the end, however, life is one big austerity in one form or another, and the first step in getting through it is simply controlling the mind and senses. That is what Krishna first teaches Arjuna. That is our first lesson, our first hurdle to overcome, our first 'new habit' to form, to develop, to nurture. Sense control is a lifelong application.

By now you should know, have experienced, should at least be able to mentally accept that exercising this control is, in every way, very much a worthwhile endeavour.

Yoga means voluntarily removing the impediments to progressing in spiritual understanding.

And this is, after all, what we are striving for, what we are obviously keen to develop if we have taken up this process of acquiring the knowledge of what yoga truly is, and how it is presented through the pages of the Gita and the *Yoga Sutras*. Voluntarily removing the impediments within the self and in one's life that may stall one's yoga practice, cause disruptions or prevent one from achieving any kind of satisfaction in one's actions, is really the only kind of austerity one needs to perform. To consciously approach life and yoga, with this voluntary mood of letting go of things that impede our growth, is how Arjuna responded to Krishna's wisdom. He willingly removed those things that impeded his progress and was able to move on, overcoming the negative emotions that had overwhelmed him.

As Krishna said to Arjuna, 'In this endeavour there is no loss or diminution, and a little advancement on this path can protect one from the most dangerous type of fear.'

CHAPTER 11

Svadhyaya

Study of the Self and the Scriptures

BEFORE WE LOOK AT the meaning of *svadhyaya*, we should understand the reason for its inclusion in Patanjali's niyamas. This word is translated as 'sva', one's own self, the human soul, and 'adhyaya', lesson. Dhyaya also means meditation, contemplation. Svadhyaya means a meditative study of the self and the sacred texts.

In dictionaries around the world, the word 'sacred' is understood to mean 'connected with God'. But does our sadhana embody the real meaning of what is sacred? Not surprisingly, the most concise answer comes from Yogacharya B.K.S. Iyengar, who has written that during the process of yoga, one starts to realize that 'all creation is meant for bhakti rather than for bhoga, enjoyment, that all creation is divine, that there is divinity within oneself, and that the energy that moves one is that same that moves the entire universe.'[1]

[1] B.K.S. Iyengar, *Light on Yoga*, Unwin Hyman, 1989.

'Yoga' means to connect to God; 'sacred' means connected with God. Yoga, by definition, is sacred.

Many words have become trite due to their exhaustive usage. One of these words is 'yogi'. B.K.S. Iyengar was a wonderful example of a yogi who depended upon and gave all credit to his predecessors and masters, and to the sacred texts and teachings that were his foundation, his very life. He was a yogi in the real sense of every word in the yamas and niyamas. So a leaf out of Mr. Iyengar's book is a good start in understanding the sacred texts that were his foundation: Patanjali's *Yoga Sutras* and even beyond that, the Bhagavad Gita.

'All creation is made for bhakti', Krishna says in chapter 14, meaning that the culmination of all sacrifices and austerities is transcendental knowledge, which is acquired from the study of sacred texts and the guidance of spiritually knowledgable people. As Krishna says to Arjuna, 'In this world, there is nothing so sublime and pure as transcendental knowledge. Such knowledge is the mature fruit of all mysticism. And one who has become accomplished in the practice of bhakti yoga enjoys this knowledge within himself in due course of time' (4:38).

Krishna's wisdom and teachings in the Gita encompass all the elements of our progress through the yamas and niyamas in a practical and constructive way that embodies not only the practice of yoga, but a deeper and more substantial understanding of how the universe works, and what our place is within the material realm. The entire understanding of our place in the universe and, most importantly, how to transcend the material energy – not simply live within it – are spelled out in a clear, progressive format that gives impetus to our yoga practice, both externally and internally.

Yoga means to understand the real self and the eternal nature of that self.

As Bhaktivedanta Swami summarizes: 'Study of the sacred texts is not meant for the recreation of armchair speculators, but for the formation of character.'

So let us proceed with our character development and move towards the final stage of the spiritual journey: the awareness of the Divine.

CHAPTER 12

Ishvara-Pranidhana

Meditation on the Supreme

The ultimate union we all seek

WE NOW ARRIVE AT the final goal of yoga, the supreme destination, the culmination of years of work: to be connected to the Divine. Of course, it is not like a train arriving at a station; we do not sit and wait patiently and suddenly have the doors open so we can step onto the platform of enlightenment!

To reach this final stage in one's spiritual journey is the work of a lifetime. The path to the Divine is a journey through years engaged in the living of each yama and niyama, and the intricate, ever-changing and complex dance that yoga is. Even before the final goal is reached – eternal devotion to the Supreme, awareness of the Divine, surrender to the Lord – arrives the tangible realization of each step we have taken.

Yet, as you understand by now, it is essential to know about ishvara-pranidhana at the very start of our yogic journey, otherwise our practice of yoga will be but an exercise regime, presented as a lifestyle choice; beneficial, no doubt, but always somehow missing the real point. Without knowing why we are practicing yoga – and what yoga is, why the yamas and niyamas need to be followed, and so on – we will not be able to proceed with our spiritual journey.

With each step we take through the foundational precepts of yoga, from the first yama to this final niyama, we understand Krishna's deeper instructions to Arjuna, which lead us through the refinement of human life and culminate in what is considered the core teaching of the Gita and one that embodies the entire practice of yoga. In chapter 18, verse 62, Krishna says to Arjuna, 'Abandon all varieties of religion and just surrender unto Me. I shall deliver you from all sinful reactions. Do not fear.'

What does it mean to be told simultaneously to surrender to the Supreme and to 'abandon all varieties of religion'?

Surrender and religion are two entirely different things: surrender is spiritual in nature, while religion is material. If, finally, our yoga practice is not centred on attaining the prime spiritual goal, then it is bound to the material realm, practised like any other religion but never quite reaching the spiritual heights we long for and that yoga is meant for.

Remember that Krishna and Arjuna engaged in this dialogue five thousand years ago. While some may think that point alone knocks it out of the ballpark in modern relatable terms, it actually takes place on the threshold of the age in which we now live, the Kaliyuga: the age of quarrel and hypocrisy. Consequently, it is tailor-made for twenty-first century residents.

But one point remains unanswered till now: in the course of his conversations with Krishna, Arjuna expresses what he believes to be the near-impossible feat of practising yoga. He says to Krishna that 'the system of yoga which You have summarized appears impractical and unendurable to me, for the mind is restless and unsteady…turbulent, obstinate and very strong, and to subdue it, I think, is more difficult than controlling the wind' (6:33–34).

In chapter 6, Krishna shares with Arjuna that it is impossible to practise this form of yogi-hood that we are so often exposed to commercially, which we are accustomed to thinking is the goal, or even assume to be an advanced practice. I am referring to those who think yoga is sitting in the lotus pose. We can sit in our Facebook-ready picture-perfect postures, poised elegantly on a rock in a calm pool of water, but it isn't long before the bottom is sore, the sun rises and starts burning our face, the stomach starts to churn with hunger, and we are forced to scramble from our lofty perch and admit that this process is a bit beyond us. So what is the point of Krishna explaining all this to Arjuna if it is impossible?

Krishna's answer always, inevitably, returns to the same point: 'As a lamp in a windless place does not waver, so the transcendentalist, whose mind is controlled, remains always steady in his meditation on the transcendent self.' He assures Arjuna that 'it is undoubtedly very difficult to curb the restless mind, but it is possible by suitable practice and by detachment' (6.35).

In other words, our path through life, our yoga practice, our ability to absorb the teachings, and the purpose of yoga and of life, all come back to what I mentioned right at the beginning of this book: control of the mind and senses.

Perhaps we think this is too flippant a response. But I'm sorry to say there are no shortcuts – this *is* the shortcut to finding any kind of equilibrium and peace. As Krishna says early on in the Gita, in chapter 2: 'One who is not connected with the Supreme can have neither transcendental intelligence nor a steady mind, without which there is no possibility of peace. And how can there be any happiness without peace?'

As we have learnt, 'connected with the Supreme' is the actual definition of yoga. So, practising yoga, learning the qualities and characteristics required to advance in yoga are, in fact, still 'yoga.' Further, they are about this niyama, ishvara-pranidhana, meditating on the Supreme.

In chapter 6 of the Gita, we have talked about Arjuna's worry about failure on the yogic path, and Krishna's response to him: 'By virtue of the divine consciousness of his previous life, he automatically becomes attracted to the yogic principles, even without seeking them' (6.44). Krishna adds that this practice of yoga, performed in an intelligent way in the mode of goodness, means that one can never fail – either in this life or the next.

Krishna also teaches that there is no loss or diminution on this path. Nothing we do is ever lost or wasted, for all the work we put it on the path to seek the Divine contributes to the ultimate goal, whenever that might occur. Further, if one falls away from the path of yoga – by choice or circumstance – they will, in this life or the next, become attracted again to the philosophy and practice of yoga, even without seeking. Such a person's life will be a far more ideal situation for pursuing the life of yoga they had sought to practise previously.

So remember: inspite of the level at which we may be in our own lives, we are assured of our attainment of this goal of yoga, and we are encouraged by the discussions between Krishna and Arjuna to draw yoga into our daily living, consciousness and behaviour.

B.K.S. Iyengar summed it up in a beautiful way and, as always, his words – while artful and melodic themselves – embody the fundamental elements of the practice he lived, breathed and taught through the unique presentation of Patanjali's Sutras and Krishna's Gita: 'Yoga is like music: the rhythm of the body, the melody of the mind, and the harmony of the soul create the symphony of life.'

So how do we attain union with the Divine? How do we live through our sadhana, our lives a symphony of the combined attributes that yoga embodies, culminating in surrender to the Supreme? Despite having already repeated the same answer over and over, it remains the same: by control of the mind and senses. This is the key to all that Krishna and Patanjali teach.

Part 3

ENTERING AN INTERNAL PRACTICE

The Last Six Limbs of Yoga

CHAPTER 1

Charting the Course of the Yogic Path

It is at this point that a more detailed and clear explanation is required of the eightfold path of yoga that makes up Patanjali's *Yoga Sutras*, and how our progress through the different stages is laid out in this handbook.

While a complete and thorough description of each limb of the eightfold process is given in both the previous section (yamas and niyamas) and the upcoming section (the last six limbs of ashtanga), there is some more detail to the stages that we need to understand before we proceed.

As we are by now fully aware, the eight limbs of yoga are yama, niyama, asana, pranayama, pratyahara, dharana, dhyana and samadhi.

However, these eight limbs are divided into two specific categories defined as external (bahiranga) and internal (antaranga).

Bahiranga

1. *Yamas*

2. *Niyamas*
3. *Asana*
4. *Pranayama*

Antaranga

1. *Pratyahara*
2. *Dharana*
3. *Dhyana*
4. *Samadhi*

After the last section, which covered the first two limbs of ashtanga yoga, yama and niyama, the third and final section is a detailed yet practical exploration of the other six limbs of yoga: asana, pranayama, pratyahara, dharana, dhyana, and samadhi.

We speak in this section of the book of entering an internal practice, yet asana and pranayama are in the bahiranga category, which is the external component of yoga. So why is it here, you may wonder, in the section that addresses our internal practice?

Certainly we could have created yet another section of the book entitled 'external yoga'. But it is unncessary and may be confusing. The reason the yamas and niyamas have their own section in the book is because they are the two limbs of ashtanga yoga that Patanjali details the most. The category they are in, bahiranga, can perhaps best be understood by calling it the 'preparatory stage' for our internal practice.

Yet, confusion may persist, for the yamas and niyamas, while in the category of bahiranga, are 'qualities'. You may wonder how character development is an 'external' practice!

As just mentioned yama and niyama, along with asana and pranayama, are the 'preparatory' stages; conversely, the antaranga stage of yoga, the internal practice, differs greatly from the learning, preparing and practising stage.

Patanjali describes pratyahara, the first limb in the antaranga stage, as the bridge that takes the yoga practitioner from the external to the internal meditations of yoga – a transitional stage that leads the practitioner from conscious learning and practice into the more internal, 'unthinking' level.

Dividing the stages of yoga into sections helps us to navigate our progress with ease, and understand what is required before moving onto the next stage. It also helps us understand what we have achieved during the observance or practice of the stages we have moved through. While technically, asana and pranayama do not strictly belong in the 'last limbs of yoga' category, it is more practical to understand a section that addresses just the yamas and niyamas.

Therefore, with this clear understanding of ashtanga yoga and its stages, let us now approach our internal practice by exploring the last two limbs in the bahiranga stage: asana and pranayama.

CHAPTER 2

Asana

Tuning the vehicle that carries the internal soul to its destination...

SO WE ARE OFF the battlefield of the Gita, and find ourselves in the midst of what Patanjali called the mindfield – the arena where we have to master the network of thoughts that make up that war zone of the mind.

The first lesson we glean from the conversation between Krishna and Arjuna is the control of the mind and senses. With Patanjali, we have the yamas and niyamas. While consisting of principles that help form and hone a refined character, the goal and consequence of practising the yamas and niyamas is the control of the mind and senses, as you have understood by now.

We have seen in the previous chapters how the Gita describes a yogi as one who has acquired equilibrium. Krishna speaks of conquering the eternal stream of opposites in chapter 6, verse 7, where he tells Arjuna, 'For one who has conquered the mind, the Supersoul is already reached, for he has attained tranquility. To such a man happiness and distress, heat and cold, honor and dishonor are all the same.' Equilibrium and balance in the face of these daily obstacles is the mark of a yogic being.

And asana is the very beginning of attaining that level of freedom from the dualities that affect us. The foundational asanas that represent solidity and steadiness – like padmasana, virasana and dandasana – are now a crucial stage of the yoga practice.

Asana has two stages. One is practising asanas – doing the poses and learning to bring the body to a stage of softness, adaptability and strength. The other is 'asana' as the preparatory stage for an advanced yoga practice.

At this point, we have the foundational aspects of yoga firmly instilled in the mind and body. The body's muscles, bones, organs, cells and tissues have actually imbibed over the course of time the science of yoga, the foundational practices that Patanjali teaches in his yamas and niyamas. Further, the matters Krishna addresses in chapter 16 in terms of diet and health, and thought, action and speech, being situated in the mode of goodness, all make up the physical practice of yoga, and this includes the actual performance of yoga.

When the body is ready and when the mind is ready,
we prepare to enter the realm of the soul; this is yoga.

While pratyahara marks the crossover point from the external practice of yoga to the internal, it cannot be reached until asana is executed in the right consciousness.

Practising asanas in the right consciousness means understanding that asana is preparing the physical body – limbs, tissues, organs, muscles, tendons, bones…each part of the body down to the very cells – to be a *vehicle* for one's yoga practice rather than the subject of it. It is at this point we can appreciate the real role of asana: the body is readily and easily positioned, not merely a lump of non-negotiable flesh and matter but a responsive, tuned vehicle that is in line with the driver within – the soul.

In the beginning stages of yoga, asana is physical. We train the body to assume certain positions and postures, and instruct the muscles and cells to remember a series of alignments. Gradually, over time, the body learns to do this with ease. The reason for this is simple: as previously mentioned, what we practise becomes second nature, and second nature gradually becomes first nature. Thus, the asanas become a vehicle for the higher stages of yoga that we set out to attain.

It is a given by now that your work in yoga has been enhanced by understanding the deep and varied meanings of yoga, by appreciating the science it is, and by the depth and breadth of the actual practice. Now, as you reach this point, it is time for a more subtle understanding of asana as the preparation for the internal practice of yoga. The body has readied itself and does not struggle to 'do' yoga but softly and swiftly moves into the asana that is most conducive to direct you to the advanced limbs of yoga. The body is no longer an obstacle. Neither are the senses now, for they have been subdued. For what is asana if not the launching pad to one's internal living of spiritual yoga? If we wanted merely lithe bodies, softened joints and developed muscles, surely a jog around the park would suffice. Or an exercise regime at the gym and an oil massage every other day. But we know that this is not what yoga is about.

Yoga is neither an exercise program nor a lifestyle choice for the health conscious.

Let's face it: 'yoga' is possibly the most prominent and explosive social phenomenon the world has ever experienced. Never in history has the world been so connected as it became in the late twentieth century, with the global village phenomenon allowing yoga to have the impact it never had before. Reaching through the diverse fields of fashion and publishing to fitness and public relations, yoga has entered and conquered every aspect of society in any way it can. You will meet any number of people who are yoga teachers or yoga students. And even for those who are neither, the word 'yoga' is now an integrated part of the English language. But, as we can clearly see from all we've learnt and imbibed through the course of Krishna's and Patanjali's teachings as outlined in this handbook, yoga is a journey of life.

I would like to reiterate at this stage that you can (and must) prevent your yogic journey from resembling a superficial path of mere exercise or a trendy lifestyle. This is precisely the 'mindfield' that Patanjali speaks of avoiding. Your path is kept free of these obstacles when the foundations to your practice are genuine, strong and performed with humility.

Yoga is really the practice of learning to serve, to please the Beloved, to take the conditioned senses beyond the material realm and lay them at the door of the Divine. We may have a long way to go before achieving such a state, but it all begins with assuming the mood, consciousness, state of being…and then assuming the position, the asana.

CHAPTER 3

Pranayama

The soul is a symptom of life, and the breath a symptom of the soul, winding through the body like a river of consciousness, uniting life with thought, action and prayer

ALTHOUGH WE ARE ENTERING the higher, more inward levels of yoga, we are still in the preparatory stages as it were, each stage qualifying us further for the final limbs of dharana, dhyana and samadhi. We have understood through the asana chapter – and this chapter on pranayama will emphasize this point further – that all of this is but foundational work for the spiritual practice of yoga. So, breathing exercises that improve the lungs, physical positions that strengthen the back or open the hips, cures for physical or mental ailments are benefits of yogic practice and are mere exercise without the transcendent goal that *is* yoga.

Yoga is the path to transcendence.

Patanjali notes in his *Yoga Sutras* that mental disturbance and despondency are symptoms of uncontrolled or artless breath, and that the science of breathing positively affects the psychological and emotional health of a person. Pranayama is the stage of our practice that counteracts these sufferings and challenges of the mind. It is not simply 'breathing' but balancing the connection between the breath, the mind, and more subtle aspects like the emotions.

As I have explained earlier, the word 'pranayama' is composed from two Sanskrit words: 'prana' meaning life force or breath; and 'ayama' meaning restraint or control. Prana is the same as the Chinese 'chi'. Qigong (pronounced 'chee-gong') is the ancient Chinese exercise and healing system that involves meditation, controlled breathing and movement. Similarly, the Japanese word 'ki' embodies the spirit or essence of movement (like air or breath) through the physical body and the subtle mind. In other words, ancient Eastern cultures and traditions have for eons understood the vital force, the breath in the body, as being the key to a healthy mind and body.

Within the field of pranayama, there are ten kinds of air:

- The main air that passes through the nose during breathing is called 'prana'.
- The air that passes through the rectum as evacuated bodily air is called 'apana'.
- The air that adjusts the food within the stomach and sometimes sounds like belching is called 'samana'.

- The air that passes through the throat, the stoppage of which constitutes suffocation, is called 'udana'.
- The total air that circulates through the entire body is called 'vyana'.

Then, there are five subtler airs:

- The air that facilitates the opening of the eyes, mouth, etc., is called 'naga'.
- The air that increases appetite is called 'kakara'.
- The air that causes contraction is called 'kurma'.
- The air that helps relaxation by opening the mouth wide (in yawning) is called 'devadatta'.
- The air that helps sustenance is called 'dhananjaya'.

So we start to understand that pranayama is indeed a science that eradicates physiological imbalance and disease. Without this stage, it is not possible to move on to the more advanced stages of yoga. Patanjali's sutras explain that the original purpose of yoga is to prepare the practitioner for spiritual advancement through the fine-tuning of the vehicle of the soul, which is the body.

In his introduction to *Light on Yoga,* B.K.S. Iyengar speaks of the four remedies given by Patanjali for reaching the higher levels of the yogic process: friendship (maitri); compassion (karuna); joy (mudita); and rejection or neglect of unfavourable qualities (upeksa). He writes, 'The deeper significance of these fourfold remedies cannot be felt by an unquiet mind....the way to achieve [that] is to work with determination on two of the eight stages of yoga mentioned by Patanjali, namely, asana and pranayama.'

To summarize, Patanjali's four remedies can only be achieved by a quiet mind, or as Krishna repeatedly states to Arjuna, one who has control of the mind and senses. With this control, the intelligence is the guide, and one can easily determine what is beneficial or harmful to one's life or yogic practice. Patanjali's yamas and niyamas include the cultivation of compassion (through non-violence) and the rejection of unfavourable qualities (austerity and abstinence). Finally, a quiet mind is acquired through working with determination on the stages of asana and pranayama.

CHAPTER 4

Pratyahara

Bridging the gap between the material and the spiritual...

PRATYAHARA MEANS WITHDRAWING THE mind and senses from external objects, a conscious closing of the mind to the pull of the senses. It is a stage of yoga practice where we stop being controlled by the mind and senses; instead, we are in control of them.

When we think of crossing a bridge, it is most often in the metaphorical sense of overcoming an obstacle, or putting something off until we reach a point when it can no longer be avoided, as in 'we will cross that bridge when we reach it'. It should come as no surprise that in yoga, the opposite is true.

Our 'bridge' here is a subtle happening, a gentle and seamless gliding into a new phase of yoga. This is the stage of pratyahara, which Patanjali describes as the bridge between bahiranga, the external aspects of yoga, and antaranga, the internal aspects.

Attaining the pratyahara stage – actually realizing it – is the key to entering the last three stages of yoga, those internal practices of dharana, dhyana and samadhi. Here, the consciousness is internalized; this is not a 'thinking' stage anymore but one where the yoga has become one's very nature, and what is initially a 'learning' and 'doing' stage is now simply the new 'normal.' The senses are withdrawn and the sensations of touch, sound, scent, taste and speech are secondary, contained by the controlled king of the senses, which is the mind.

Withdrawing the senses is something of a misnomer. It is not that we are engaging in shutting down or repressing the senses. In fact, at this stage, they are sharper, more attuned and refined than ever before, but they are perfectly *controlled*. Early in the Gita (2.58), Arjuna asks Krishna, 'What are the symptoms of one whose consciousness is merged in transcendence?' Krishna replies: 'One who is able to withdraw his senses from sense objects, as the tortoise draws its limbs within the shell, is firmly fixed in perfect consciousness.'

When we are more drawn to the internal pull of the soul than we are to the external tugging of the senses, we can truly say we have reached the level of pratyahara, where the 'sadhana' is now guided by something higher than the mind, senses and even the intelligence. Yes, of course, the intelligence has led us here, but it cannot take us any further. It, too, must be surrendered. As I have already mentioned, this is not a 'thinking' stage.

How do we know we are no longer susceptible to the lure of the senses?

Yoga practitioners in the early stages or even the more advanced spiritual stages often ask why they feel impelled to indulge in the senses when they don't actually want to. Engaging the senses freely in the objects of gratification is most often an instinctual response to situations that frighten or threaten us. It is easy for the conditioned mind and senses to remain fixed in the behavioural patterns that are familiar, despite wanting to move out of them. In fact, the senses will throw all sorts of obstacles at us to lure us away from the path of renunciation and peace, and continue to drag us down the path of repeated sense gratification.

Yoga is the practice that peels away the layers of conditioning in the mind, psyche, emotions and body.

And the senses are powerful, the greatest enemy of the yoga practitioner. The Upanishads describe the body as a chariot and the senses as its horses – an analogy that helps us understand more deeply the use of the words 'rein in' and 'control' in terms of the mind and senses. The Vedas speak of a most advanced and renounced yogi, Yamunacharya, whose now-famous revelation was, 'Since I have been engaged in bhakti-yoga, whenever I think of sex life my face at once turns from it and I spit at the thought.'

The most telling detail of this statement is not that he turned away from the temptations of sex, but that even as an advanced and renounced yogi his mind and senses were still assailed by thoughts of sex from time to time. In other words, we are never going to be free of the senses, but we can be free of the impure state of mind and the endless struggle with pointless and regret-filled indulgence. It is the ability to make a choice, using our intelligence to drive us, that matters here. Therefore, yoga is not about denying the senses artificially, but directing them properly.

Yoga allows one to harness the senses with the reins of intelligence.

Therefore, Arjuna's lesson on the battlefield is how to direct the senses so that they are used for the proper reasons: his objection to killing, to engaging in war, his telling Krishna 'I will not fight' all are overcome by his mind being redirected. He is finally able to make a choice – that he *will* fight – and for the right reasons.

Arjuna does not shut his senses down, harden his heart or repress his natural response to the demands of war; he does not become oblivious and insensitive to everything and everyone around him. He simply redirects his senses toward their supreme engagement – bhakti yoga, service with devotion.

Thus, the senses will never cease to stake their claim on the body and the mind, as Arjuna and Yamunacharya teach us. But as one advances on the path of yoga, one learns to focus on the nature of the goal of yoga. The result is that sensory demands become secondary and elicit no response from the deeper self. This is what detachment really is.

We have read earlier that yoga is the practice that teaches the intelligence to be guided by a process superior to the mind and senses. And here we have arrived at that place. But what is next? Who, or what, will lead us to the next limb?

Yoga is the science of transcending the physical and attaining the ethereal, of using something deeper than the external senses to perceive.

This is a crucial lesson the Bhagavad Gita is giving us: we can live in this world of ours, with all its material advantages and temptations, with all its tragedies and traumas, and we can still find that inner stillness by learning to work on ourselves: working on the mind; addressing fears, worries and anxieties; and confronting and undoing conditioning at many levels.

CHAPTER 5

Dharana

Leaving the mind and senses behind, we enter the first of the internal stages of yoga…

WE NOW ARRIVE AT the transitional stage of our practice, when that which has gone before is now realized as preparative, and that which comes after is understood as entering into the deeper practice of yoga.

Yoga means seeing that all we do is simply preparation for…yoga.

The transition from pratyahara or the withdrawal of the senses to mastering the senses, consciously turning one's energy away from being controlled by the senses to being controlled by the intelligence, and internalizing concentration – this is dharana. It is a harnessing of all that we have gained control of and conquered, a conscious focusing toward the next step, which is the stage of dhyana, meditation. In a sense, dharana is the beginning stage of meditation, but it is a transitional phase: it is on its way somewhere, and we are in charge of where it goes – or if it goes at all.

In fact, it is a little difficult to separate these last three stages of yoga: concentration, meditation and absorption. Patanjali explains them collectively in his sutras as a process in and of themselves. While they are entered into individually, they each represent a third of the combined final stage of yoga, and are thus referred to as samyama, which Patanjali says is *trayam ekatra samyama*: trayam (the three), ekatra (as one), samyama (dharana, dhyana, and samadhi).

We all know what it is to concentrate: school/university exams, sewing clothes for our children, running a company, decorating a room, writing a book, planting a garden, or cooking. All require a concentrated effort, an engagement of the senses, a focused direction of the physical and mental abilities. From these experiences, we can actually understand how the internal practice of yoga begins.

> *Yoga means consciously directing the energy in the body, not simply moving the limbs like a tree moves its branches.*

And this is where the process of dharana is engaged, where the practice not only *becomes* internal but *stems from* an internal understanding of yoga, of all we have done to arrive at this point. Think of how it is just not possible to suddenly walk into an exam room and write an exam without having attended classes and without preparing for it.

Yoga is not an acquirement; it is a process.

If you have not yet reached this meditative stage of the yoga process, then your movements are merely movements. In the early stages of your practice, all your movements are applied movements, in that they come from an external source and are applied to the body: you look at your teacher, you see what is required, your brain sends an instruction to your body, and you 'do' yoga.

This process can be likened to a cutting from a tree: you can take the physical representation of that tree – the cutting – and plant it in the ground. Yet, a seed planted in the ground will slowly take root and, in time, will produce the external effect. A cutting, however, may appear to have produced a form but actually the form came first, and its process of finding roots and developing are an after-effect of being planted.

If we approach yoga in the latter way – that is, first adopting the form and then trying to establish roots – we simply do not enter into dharana. We must approach it in the former manner: plant the seed, nurture it, wait for the roots to take, and then appreciate the plant and the flowering. We begin at the beginning, slowly acquire knowledge through study and practice, and *then* see the fruit of our early endeavours. This is how we move past the external application of knowledge or the 'seeing and doing' stage of yoga and enter the realm of realized knowledge.

At the stage of dharana, form takes a back seat to principle, and the subtle takes over: we are qualified, we have mastered control, and we are ready for the next stage of meditation, dhyana.

CHAPTER 6

Dhyana

Yoga steps off the mat and into the realm of the sacred…

DHYANA IS THE UNINTERRUPTED flow of concentration. Although concentration (dharana) and meditation (dhyana) appear to be similar, there is a fine yet distinct line that separates them. Where dharana requires one-pointed attention, dhyana is contemplative and reflective, like a river: a stream of continuous thought, a current of contemplation, a flow of awareness.

As we progress through the stages of yoga as they are presented here in chapter form and from the beginning through to the internal practice where we are now, we can see that we have gone from 'doing' and have started the 'entering' stage. It is here that we comprehend how yoga is a process and not something one achieves. We have learnt this through the practice we have engaged in as we have gone through the various stages.

Progressing through the stages of yoga, with our practice maturing, we may not be conscious of it but we lose the idea that we are reaching for a goal or trying to acquire a qualification or a level: we are just there, in our practice. And that is the level that qualifies us first for dharana, and now for dhyana.

However, here is where we reach an intellectual shift: B.K.S. Iyengar says of these three stages of yoga – the samyama stage of dharana, dhyana, and samadhi – that they are experiencing stages, for while asana and pranayama can be 'explained, taught, shown and corrected', samyama has to be experienced.

Patanjali refers to thought in his *Yoga Sutras* as 'vritti', waves that rise then recede, rise then recede. While dharana is a state of mind, a still and introspective concentration, dhyana, he says, is the unbroken flow, a non-stop wave of thought directed toward the object of meditation, thought uninterrupted by mental roadblocks or diversions. It is yoga in the state of being, not in the state of doing or thinking.

The state of being means a state where mental analysis has ceased. All those times, so many years ago, when we 'thought' we were 'doing' yoga, we can now look back at our progress through our practice and be grateful for what is now a way of life, not just a daily activity. We cannot see any difference anymore between our yoga practice and our life practice, because there is none.

One engages in yoga initially according to one's lifestyle, schedule, need, ability and desire. Over time, it becomes an unchangeable aspect of one's life, not merely an inclusion in the day but the day itself.

Yoga means applying our practice to every moment of our day.

It is at this stage that we enter the transitional level of dharana. We have reached here, and now that focused energy is part of us – it is not something we do but is something we *are*, something we turn to both consciously and sub-consciously. It is a part of our nature…in fact, it has become our nature.

Yoga is the nature that supercedes our conditioning.

Everything now is realized. Those who have reached a mature level of practice are not reading these words and mentally storing them in the vault marked 'future', for it is already recognizable, everything we think and see and feel is now part of our yoga nature.

And B.K.S. Iyengar – or anyone associated with his practices – never taught samyama. It is a process that cannot be discussed or taught, but must simply be experienced or entered into by the individual practitioner when qualified.

In fact, there are yoga practitioners who demand a mystical experience, meditative bliss or instant enlightenment as a reward for their yoga practice! According to B. K. S. Iyengar, this is disrespectful and abusive to the yoga process, a 'dangerous form of immaturity' and damaging not only to the body but to the mind as well.

We now go into chapter 6 of the Bhagavad Gita, entitled 'Dhyana-yoga', where Krishna tells Arjuna, 'For one who is a neophyte in the eightfold yoga system, work is said to be the means; and for one who is already elevated in yoga, cessation of all material activities is said to be the means.' Cessation does not mean sitting in the Himalayas in the lotus position and doing nothing but meditating. If we are advanced in our practice, we have already entered the stage of cessation: cessation of the senses, harnessing them via the intelligence, internalizing our practice and *being* rather than doing.

Yoga means connecting with the Supreme.

It is at this stage that we realize that dhyana-yoga, as described by Krishna in the Gita and Patanjali in his *Yoga Sutras*, means meditating on the form of the Lord. *This* is what everything until now has been leading to, not health, balance, equilibrium, control of the senses for peace, or a yoga body. No. It is about being able to meditate on the Lord. This is not personal choice, religion or anything else: it is not even yoga practice. It is life.

Yoga means life, and life means service to the Supreme Lord.

The preparative stage is over. And now we reach the point where Krishna tells Arjuna that from here on, an intellectual engagement in the yoga process is *useless*. I'll repeat that: from the stage of dharana onwards, the yoga process is intellectually impenetrable.

Krishna explains to Arjuna how one attains perfection through yoga, and Arjuna's response is 'the system of yoga which You have summarized appears impractical and unendurable to me' (6.33). It is undeniable that the process of yoga in this day and age is a ridiculously impossible goal to achieve. Yet, Arjuna finds this process no less arduous in his time! As he says '...the mind is restless and unsteady, turbulent, obstinate and very strong, and to subdue it, I think, is more difficult than controlling the wind.' Krishna replies that 'it is possible by suitable practice and by detachment' . Then he tells Arjuna what an actual yogi is: '[Yoga] perfection is characterised by one's ability to see the Self by the pure mind and to relish and rejoice in the Self. In that joyous state, one is situated in boundless transcendental happiness, realized through transcendental senses' (6:33–35).

This is where, if your goal has not been to link with the Supreme, you need to either quit your yoga practice or go back to a certain point where you can understand that all you were doing till now was simply to prepare yourself to meet the Divine.

So is the mind pure? Is the mind fixed on Krishna? Is there still something telling you that this is not the goal of yoga, that you did not set out on this path seeking God but instead wanted equilibrium and holistic well-being? If that is what you were taught at the beginning, then you have been cheated. Krishna tells Arjuna, 'A true yogi observes Me in all beings and also sees every being in Me. Indeed, the self-realized person sees Me, the same Supreme Lord, everywhere.'

Krishna explains to Arjuna that it is divine consciousness that one needs to develop further at this stage; if this is not the goal then one's sadhana is incomplete. But then, Krishna makes a very interesting point. The fact that we are all drawn to yoga practices is, according to him, already evidence that we are seeking this divine consciousness, even without knowing. Krishna tells Arjuna, 'By virtue of the divine consciousness of his previous life, he automatically becomes attracted to the yogic principles – even without seeking them' (6.44).

He tells Arjuna, 'Be a yogi,' and summarizes with the words, 'And of all yogis, the one with great faith who always abides in Me, thinks of Me within himself, and renders transcendental loving service to Me – he is the most intimately united with Me in yoga and is the highest of all. That is My opinion.'

Unless you haven't realized it yet, we are now officially and completely off the mat.

'One should make me the ultimate goal of life.'

Welcome to yoga...

CHAPTER 7

Samadhi

Leaving behind the mind, senses and the intellect, now we enter the realm of the soul

PATANJALI DESCRIBES THIS EIGHTH and final stage of ashtanga, samadhi, as a state of ecstasy. At this stage the yoga practitioner realizes a profound union with the Divine. The Vedic dictionary, the *Nirukti*, says *samyag adhiyate 'sminn atma-tattva-yathatmyam*: 'When the mind is fixed for understanding the self, it is said to be in samadhi.' Samadhi is, in short, the ultimate goal of one's yoga practice.

By now, the practitioner has reached the understanding that nothing can be acquired through borrowed intelligence. B.K.S. Iyengar says 'Using somebody else's words and then saying you are practising yoga is what I call being a carbon copy. It is borrowed intelligence. Borrowed intelligence cannot become meditation.' In that case, this chapter should perhaps be a blank page. There are, in truth, few words to explain the stage of samadhi as part of the yoga process, a process that now no longer exists in a tangible form. We cannot enter into dharana, dhyana or samadhi with the power of the intellect, the mind or the senses, nor refer to a written guide, a how-to manual.

All other yogas are but means to come to the point of bhakti.

So, at the earlier stages of our yoga practice – be it one year ago or thirty years ago – when we are reading of the future of our practice and what it should look like or will look like, we set out to acquire this standard. Now, at this level, there is no striving or achieving. In his summation to the fifth chapter in the Gita, Bhaktivedanta Swami writes, 'There is a gradual process of elevation in the practice of yama, niyama, asana, pranayama, pratyahara, dharana, dhyana and samadhi. But these are merely the preface to perfection, which can only be attained by bhakti, the highest perfection of life which alone can award peace to the human being.'

As we have engaged in this gradual process of elevation, through constant work and dedication we begin to understand the depth and breadth of yoga, and how much it will take to actually reach the higher stages of the process.

The culmination of all kinds of yoga practices lies in bhakti yoga.

Samadhi means to be absolutely and purely in complete consciousness of the Supreme Lord, towards whom our entire life practice has been directed. In chapter 2 of the Gita, Krishna explains to Arjuna, 'When your mind is no longer disturbed by the flowery language of the Vedas, and when it remains fixed in the trance of self-realization, then you will have attained the divine consciousness.' This is the goal of yoga Krishna is speaking of: this is samadhi.

So are we there yet? And if we are, what does it look like? In response to Krishna's description of a person in samadhi, Arjuna asks this very question in verse 54 of chapter 2: 'What are the symptoms of one whose consciousness is thus merged in transcendence? How does he speak, and what is his language? How does he sit, and how does he walk?'

Right here is a telling point: to ask what the symptoms are of one in samadhi, to ask what his speech, posture, and carriage resemble, indicates that Arjuna is aware that samadhi is not confined to a trance-like state, that a person in divine consciousness is, to all intents and purposes, a fully-functioning human being and not a yogi who has renounced life.

In answer to Arjuna's question, Krishna says, 'When a man gives up all varieties of desire for sense gratification, which arise from mental concoction, and when his mind, thus purified, finds satisfaction in the self alone, then he is said to be in pure transcendental consciousness.' Krishna is simply emphasizing the symptoms of the stage of samadhi.

Yoga means concentration of the mind detached from all other subject matter. Such concentration is samadhi.

So if, as Krishna explains and the Vedic dictionary defines, samadhi is not merely sitting in trance, then, as Arjuna asks, what *does* it look like? Krishna has told us what happens when one has given up the qualities that will hold us back, but we still want to know how it looks, how we identify it in another, what form it takes.

The *Srimad-Bhagavatam* has been referred to sufficiently within these pages that it needs no further introduction. It is a more elaborate and expansive treatise on the philosophical tenets of spiritual subjects, and gives more refined and detailed explanations. In the first volume, Bhaktivedanta Swami explains samadhi thoroughly yet succinctly in his commentaries in more detail than either Krishna or the *Nirukti*: 'Such a yogi devotee of the Lord engages himself twenty-four hours daily in the service of the Lord so that his whole attention is engrossed with the thoughts of the Lord in the ninefold process of devotional service, namely hearing, chanting, remembering, worshipping, praying, becoming a voluntary servant, carrying out orders, establishing a friendly relationship, or offering all that one may possess in the service of the Lord. By such practice of yoga, or linking up in the service of the Lord, one is recognized by the Lord Himself, as it is explained in the *Bhagavad Gita* concerning the highest perfectional stage of *samadhi*.' (SB 1.9.23)

Yet, Patanjali explains in his *Yoga Sutras* that at this level, knowledge 'goes beyond inference and scriptures'. So does this mean we dispense with our sources of knowledge, that these references to the Bhagavad Gita, the *Srimad-Bhagavatam* and *Nirukti* – paradoxically, even the *Yoga Sutras* themselves – are less important than what one feels, perceives or experiences?

Yes, in a way. But it is not like climbing a ladder up to the roof and then turning around and kicking the ladder away, saying 'I am on the roof, I don't need you anymore!' The qualities of gratitude and humility instilled in us through the process of our yoga practice to date give us the understanding that we could not have reached the roof without the ladder. We are grateful to that ladder, and we respect always its role in where we are. This may be a limited analogy, but it is the same with scriptural knowledge or inference: they are an inseparable part of the process, the foundation. So while our knowledge or advancement at this point goes beyond inference and scripture, it is simultaneously not without it either.

Yoga, as you know by now, was created as a process to elevate the mind, body and senses towards union with the Divine. Its purpose is spiritual. Its goal is bhakti. It is at this point, again, that the spiritual gauntlet is thrown before the yoga practitioner. Is one's goal in life to be eternally happy, find fulfilment, be life conscious, soul conscious, God conscious? Now we perhaps sense a loud, deep, yet subtle crack in the earth of the yoga community as it is divided in its answer – perhaps more than half on the side of yoga as a health and lifestyle fad, less on the side of attaining the spiritual heights that are yoga's sole purpose, by-products not withstanding.

This is the choice of the individual. But let me share again with you perhaps the most powerful verse in terms of yoga in the Gita, which is from chapter 4: 'Therefore the doubts which have arisen in your heart out of ignorance should be slashed by the weapon of knowledge. Armed with yoga, Arjuna, stand and fight.'

Arjuna is presented with a choice. You too, have a choice. But driven by the ego and the mind, one does not have the right to call their exercise and lifestyle option 'yoga' when it is not. It is not yours: it is Krishna's, the originator of yoga, and Patanjali's, the father of yoga, and it is not open to the interpretations of a conditioned mind. The ego, mind and senses will never carry one through the latter stages of the internal yoga process. The ego, mind and senses are defeated and controlled in the yoga process by the higher intelligence, which is guided by the soul.

As I've suggested earlier, for some, this is easily acceptable as their practice has always been on this trajectory; for others, it may mean back-pedalling a couple of stages, reminding themselves of what they are doing, and resetting their course; for still others, it may mean going back to the beginning and approaching the yoga process armed with knowledge and a renewed sense of purpose. Then there are those for whom it will be a sign to fight for their 'rights' to practise an exercise regime that merely resembles yoga and the concurrent right to call it yoga. This is not, however, the kind of 'armed with yoga, stand and fight' that Krishna was speaking of. Again, the choice is yours. And this time, it is Shakespeare who sums it up: 'To thine own self be true...'

These discussions belong to the stage of asana, yet we can all experience that while we may have appreciated such explanations, or relished them as new information for which we were, at the time, definitely hungry, still we were nowhere near being able to grasp such topics. We are all experiencing in our yoga practice at one point or another the one-step-forward-two-steps-back program, yet always moving forward.

We need only remember that such forward movement is dependent on the willingness to surrender the ego, mind and senses. Only then will we ever enter that realm of the soul that is the residence of true yoga because yoga, and life, are both dynamic, never still but always moving. Our only challenge is to make sure we're moving in the right direction.

May your yoga practice always lead you in the right direction!

Om tat sat.